**SCHOLASTIC**

# Creating a
# Bully-Free
# Classroom

BY CAROL S. McMULLEN

NEW YORK • TORONTO • LONDON • AUCKLAND • SYDNEY
MEXICO CITY • NEW DELHI • HONG KONG • BUENOS AIRES

Teaching
Resources

*This book is dedicated to the many wonderful children, parents, and colleagues I've worked with over the years, and to my husband, family, and friends, who have always believed in me.*

Cover design by Maria Lilja
Cover photo © Ariel Skelley/Corbis
Interior design by Melinda Belter
Illustrations by Jason Robinson
ISBN: 0-439-59024-8

1 2 3 4 5 6 7 8 9 10    40    11 10 09  08 07 06 05

# Contents

# Introduction

BULLIES HAVE BEEN A PART OF LIFE SINCE TIME IMMEMORIAL. Everyone has been bullied, and if we're honest with ourselves, most of us have bullied others at some point in our lives.

Our society is constantly inundated with examples of bullying behavior. News broadcasts, television programs, music videos, and movies all provide myriad examples of how to bully and very few examples of appropriate ways of handling bullying situations. Because violent, aggressive behavior surrounds us, we should not be particularly surprised when we see these same behaviors in our classrooms and on the playground.

In the past few years, more attention has been focused on this issue as parents and educators begin to fully realize the negative impact bullying has upon students and school environments. Is this because bullying incidents are becoming more violent? Possibly. What people are beginning to acknowledge is that bullying is a form of violence and the time has come to deal with the issue directly and in school settings.

Although it's usually older students who make the news when severe bullying incidents come to light, even primary-grade educators are seeking ways to introduce the idea of bully-proofing to young students. Why so? Bullying behaviors can be seen the moment students enter school—and what better time to teach children effective strategies to deal with bullies than at the beginning of their school careers.

It's important to catch bullying behaviors at an early stage. With proper monitoring and support, we can redirect young students and prevent them from getting attention and feelings of power—pay-offs that reinforce bullying. At the same time, we can help bullied children recognize their strengths and develop strategies to deal more successfully with bullies. Teaching students appropriate interpersonal skills affords us an opportunity to make a difference before behaviors harden into self-defeating and possibly dangerous patterns.

The ideas and activities in this book come from my experience in primary classrooms over twenty years. Supported by research and practice, the activities and strategies I've developed are based upon the essential premise that all children—bullies and bullied alike—benefit from specific lessons that stress problem-solving skills, recognizing and using

> Bullying doesn't happen in isolation; it occurs when many factors come together to produce an environment that supports it. As teachers and administrators, we have the power to create environments that promote community, acceptance, and justice and actively deny bullies power. School environments that support developing all children's self-esteem and strengths are one key to combating bullying.

personal strengths, and developing skills for relating successfully with others.

In *Creating a Bully-Free Classroom,* I've grouped these activities and strategies into four units (the "Big Four"). Each of these units is a cornerstone for creating a successful bully-proofing plan that you can adapt to meet the specific needs of your classroom community. And while the beginning of the year offers a perfect opportunity to initiate this work, the units may be introduced at any time of the year and then consistently revisited throughout the rest of the term.

**No More Bullies!** and **You Have the Power!** form the first and core unit. The goal of this unit is to help children become proactive and draw on their areas of strength to find solutions to bullying situations. In this unit, children are given opportunities to discuss, plan, and practice skills that will best help them prevent, avoid, or stop bullying. Children learn about the differences between bullying and everyday conflict. The activities and strategies introduced help children answer big questions about bullying such as *Who are bullies? Why are people bullied? What can you do when you see someone else being intimidated? Should you get involved? Where does bullying tend to take place?*

The second unit, **Marvelous Me,** offers a wonderful way for children to discover and celebrate their unique strengths and abilities and share these talents with others. The strategies and activities in this unit are geared toward developing self-esteem—encouraging children to say to themselves, "I can do this. I can handle this." Seeing oneself as being successful at something provides a huge boost in confidence, particularly for those children who are vulnerable to bullying. Students also learn that hard work, perseverance, and trying new approaches are ingredients in a recipe that builds confidence. And confident students who know they can handle new challenges are difficult to pick on!

**Fabulous Friends** is the third unit in this bully-free framework. As adults, we tend to assume that children naturally know how to be friends with others, but often they need specific information and guidance—time to talk, think, and explore the "how-to's" of being a friend. The strategies and activities in this unit focus on three essential factors for building successful relationships: respect, tolerance, and empathy. Children who bully often lack the interest or ability to "walk in someone else's shoes," and need explicit support and coaching to develop these behaviors. By creating opportunities for your students to recognize and practice these traits, you allow them to become aware of the positive feelings that successful, confident people have when they deal with others.

Of course, conflict rears its ugly head wherever people are together, and giving children the tools to deal with conflict effectively is a key part of anti-bullying work in the classroom. **Conflict Resolution**, the final unit in this book, presents a structured three-step resolution model that helps students resolve conflicts in the classroom. Using this model, children practice solving problems with their peers. They become skilled at identifying the main issue, calmly discussing it, and working together to come up with a resolution that is satisfactory to everyone involved. As a teacher, you become a coach, rather than the "resolver/enforcer" of problems in your classroom. With the exception of very serious conflict situations that require you to step in, conflict-resolution work in your classroom can enable every child to comfortably and confidently talk out problems and take ownership of the problem-solving process.

Developing a whole-school policy on bullying is another very important step in the bully-proofing process. Administrators can lead the way in supporting all students and teachers in tackling the problem of bullying, so that everyone in the community knows the language, expectations about behavior, and consequences of bullying. Chapter 8, written for teachers and administrators, presents detailed strategies for developing a clear mandate for your school.

At the end of the book, you will find a list of literature that supports the activities in each unit and helps you tie in reading comprehension with your bully-proofing work.

● ● ●

While we may never completely eliminate bullying in our classrooms, schools, and communities, we can make a critical difference by giving our children the tools and skills that will help them feel more confident. We can help them learn to recognize a bullying situation and then act in strategic ways to solve the problem.

By dealing with this issue openly in our classrooms and schools, and helping children to realize that there are many options for dealing with bullies, we go a long way toward achieving our complementary goals— ensuring that all children feel safe and happy at school and improving the learning environment.

**CHAPTER 1**

# Is Bullying a Problem in My Classroom?

*This chapter presents research findings on bullying, gives helpful definitions for bullying behaviors and the roles children and adults assume in bullying situations, and makes a case for addressing the problem of bullying directly with yourself and the children in your classroom.*

The note was in my mailbox when I arrived that Monday morning. I glanced at it and sighed. It was from one of my student's parents, Mrs. Lewis, asking me to call her about an incident involving her son Ben and another student, Chad. I already suspected what the call would be about. Chad had been harassing Ben since the beginning of the school year a few weeks before and in spite of my warnings, things had apparently not improved.

I was right. Chad had sworn at Ben and pushed him down at recess before taking his recess snack. "I didn't know anything about it," I said, frustrated.

"I think Ben feels that there's no point in telling you," Mrs. Lewis replied. "He tried to get help from you before, but he says Chad is still bullying him. He feels pretty hopeless about all this, and he's starting to kick up a fuss about coming to school. I don't know what to do. I may try and contact Chad's parents but I think you need to do something. After all, that's what you're there for, aren't you?"

After assuring her that I would try my best, I hung up and pondered the situation. I had become involved, but maybe I hadn't done enough. Obviously, my warnings and discussions with Chad had had little effect.

I realized, too, that I had not really been paying attention to the children who were being bullied. Telling Ben to avoid Chad was obviously not working, and it was becoming clear that I had to do something, and quickly, or the whole tenor of my class would be affected by a few kids. With twenty-nine active new second graders in the room, I had hoped that things would work themselves out and settle down after a few weeks. It was not to be.

This moment was a turning point for me—my frustration and desire to put an end to this behavior compelled me to learn more about bullying and the possible solutions. I had to try something new.

## The Facts About Bullying

Recent studies show that bullying is an issue of increasing importance for schools and the community at large. The statistics are startling and over-whelming. The American Academy of Child and Adolescent Psychiatry reports that "as many as half of all children are bullied at some time during their school years, and at least 10% are bullied on a regular basis" (2001). A study in the *Canadian Journal of School Psychology* found that within a total school population, it's estimated that 10 percent are bullies, anywhere from 10 to 15 percent are bullied and the rest are bystanders—children who witness bullying. They either join in or are unable to step in and stop the harassment (2001).

The same study also reveals that while the severity of bullying incidents tends to increase in middle school, younger children are just as frequently bullied as older students. To me, this underscores the importance of dealing with this issue with children in the early grades, before the behaviors become patterns and before the situation becomes dangerous.

Another study, quoted by Kathy Noll (2003), reports that 43 percent of students surveyed were fearful of going into school bathrooms. That statistic certainly rang true for me; I had a few children who were reluctant to use the bathroom unless accompanied by a friend—a practice I discouraged. The study data made me rethink the routine. I had always assumed these children were fearful of getting lost, or just wanted to spend time (a lot of time!) with a friend, but I began to see their request for a companion in a new light.

*Studies reveal that while the severity of bullying incidents tends to increase in middle school, younger children are just as frequently bullied as older students.*

The same report provides another startling statistic: every seven minutes, a child is bullied. In 4 percent of these situations adults intervene, peers intervene in 11 percent of the situations; and in 85 percent of the situations no intervention occurs. That was shocking to me. Were the incidents seen by adults but not acted upon? I realized that these numbers confirmed what bullied children have been saying, loud and clear, for a long time. I remembered Mrs. Lewis's words on the phone: *I think Ben feels there's no point in telling you. He tried to get help from you before, but he says Chad is still bullying him. He feels pretty hopeless.*

In fact, research points to negative psychological effects on bullied children who deal with the problem in isolation. The *Canadian Journal of School Psychology* study explains, "Victims of bullies report a variety of difficulties such as panic, irritability, poor concentration. . . . In its most severe forms, bullying can produce depression, feelings of hopelessness and even suicide." (2001).

While many bullied children turn their fear, frustration, and rage inward, some turn their anger into action. School shootings can be a highly visible result of bullying. The United States Secret Service released a report on preventing school shootings, saying, "In a number of cases, bullying played a key role in the decision to attack. A number of attackers had experienced bullying and harassment that were long-standing and severe. In those cases, the experience of bullying appeared to play a major role in motivating the attack at school. Bullying was not a factor in every case, and clearly not every child who is bullied in school will pose a risk. However, in a number of cases, attackers described experiences of being bullied in terms that approached torment" (2000).

**CHAPTER 1**

The tragic events of April 20, 1999, at Columbine High School in Littleton, Colorado, intensified the focus on the bullying problem, even though it has never been clearly established that bullying was the sole reason for the school shootings. The attack sparked many reports and investigations, looking for solutions to bullying in schools. A common thread emerged and was summed up well by Alicia Caldwell: ". . . while not every child pushed around in school is going to exact violent revenge, the abusive treatment of students by their peers is recognized not only as a widespread problem but a dangerous one" (2004).

While the Columbine massacre is the obvious example, *Chicago Sun Times* reporter Bill Dedman's summary of a 2000 Secret Service study of 41 school shooters points to many other incidents involving bullied children who sought revenge against their tormentors:

- On February 1, 1997, Evan Ramsey, a 16-year-old student in Bethel, Alaska, walked into his high school with a gun and killed a student and the principal. He had been bullied by other boys, had complained to the school administration, and was frustrated when they hadn't acted.

- In December, 1997, a 14-year-old boy named Joseph "Colt" Todd shot two students in Stamps, Arkansas. He said he was humiliated by the teasing he endured at school.

- In Moses Lake, Washington, in 1996, Barry Loukaitis, also 14, walked into his algebra class and killed his teacher and two students. He had said, "Some day, people are going to regret teasing me."

- School shootings are not a new phenomenon; in 1987 a student teased for his chubbiness, Nathan Ferris, shot his tormentor and then killed himself in DeKalb, Missouri. And in 1985, James Kearbey of Goddard, Kansas, killed four people at his junior high school. He said that he'd been bullied and beaten by students for years. (2000)

These examples are significant because they all point to the same things. Bullying is common in our schools and is often not taken seriously by teachers, administrators, and other adults. The consequences for bullied children can be devastating not only for them personally, but for the community at large. The question becomes not *if* we should do something, but *what* will we do to break this cycle of violence and despair?

Barbara Coloroso writes in *The Bully, the Bullied, and the Bystander*, "Breaking the cycle of violence involves more than merely identifying and stopping the bully. It requires that we examine why and how a child becomes a bully or the target of a bully (and sometimes both) as well as the role bystanders play in perpetuating the cycle. A deadly combination is a bully who gets what he wants from his target; a bullied child who is afraid to tell; bystanders who either watch, participate in the bullying, or look away; and adults who discount bullying as teasing, not tormenting; as a necessary part of growing up, not an impediment along the way, as 'boys will be boys,' not the predatory aggression that it is."

I could see some of my beliefs reflected in her statement. Didn't I really think that bullying is a part of growing up, and children should just learn to deal with it? Wasn't everyone teased?

Some common perceptions about bullying appear in the Bullying: True or False? box at right. Take a moment to identify which statements you agree with.

As I discovered through my research, all of these statements are false. I was startled by how much I had bought into some of these common misconceptions and how faulty some of my information was. It confirmed that I needed to change my whole approach toward children who bully, children who are bullied, and the children who stand by and allow it to take place.

First, I needed to know more about bullies. Could I predict who would be a bully in my classroom? What kinds of behaviors would be classified as bullying? Why did some children bully others repeatedly?

## What Is a Bully?

Bullies are people who rely on aggression and power to control others. They very carefully target their victims, choosing people who are vulnerable in some way. In his article "Bullying in Schools" (2000), Ron Banks punctures another myth. He found there is little evidence that bullies have low self-esteem. In fact, bullies tend to have overblown self-confidence and an exaggerated sense of self-worth. They have little interest in others' needs and find it difficult to take responsibility for their behavior. Children who bully often feel the victim "deserved it" or "asked for it" in some way.

Bullying behaviors take many forms. Physical and verbal aggression, taunts, threats, put-downs, social isolation—the list goes on and on. Examples of bullying and violence, so pervasive in television, movies,

---

**BULLYING: TRUE OR FALSE?**

• Bullying is just a part of growing up.

• Boys bully more often than girls.

• Bullies don't usually have any friends.

• Ignoring bullies often works.

• If children fight back, bullies will leave them alone.

• Bullies do poorly in school.

• Bullies tend to be bigger physically than other children.

• Bullies pick their victims indiscriminately.

• Children who look different always become targets of bullies.

• Bullies learn from parents who bully.

• Name-calling or teasing is not really bullying.

• Kids who bully often feel sorry for hurting other children afterward.

**CHAPTER 1**

video games, and music today, can influence bullying behavior. Teasing is often a hidden form of bullying. The bully may protest, "But I was just fooling around. I was just joking. I didn't mean it." However, the excuse doesn't lessen the impact on the child who was the target.

Children who bully come from many different socioeconomic backgrounds and family situations. Bullies come in all shapes, sizes, ages, and intellectual abilities. Many adults live or work with bullies. Sometimes bullies are victims themselves. Frequently, bullies have friends who tend to encourage and even model the bullying behaviors. Groups of bullies are also common—children seek power and safety in numbers.

> Any action that gives power to one child and hurts, humiliates, or diminishes another is bullying.

Children with Attention Deficit/Hyperactivity Disorder (AD/HD) may also exhibit bullying behaviors, but this often doesn't have as much to do with a desire for power as it does with an inability to respond appropriately to the social cues of their peers. Children with attention disorders are often impulsive and may frequently exhibit behaviors that are irritating to others. They may resort to bullying, taunting, or aggression simply to get the attention of other children, hoping that somehow they will become part of a group. A higher proportion of males than females are diagnosed with AD/HD.

In general boys are thought to be aggressors more often than girls, and traditionally they have displayed different behaviors: boys tend to be more physically aggressive and violent; girls tend to bully verbally and socially. That is, girls use exclusion, emotional abuse (taunting, starting rumors), and extortion as their weapons of choice. Recent reports and studies of violence by girls, however, indicate that girls' aggressive behaviors may be increasing (Federal Bureau of Investigation, 2003).

## Isn't It Normal to Be Bullied?: Conflict Versus Bullying

It's important to define the difference between bullying and conflict. Often the lines between the two are blurred, which reinforces the misconception that bullying is normal and children should toughen up and learn to deal with it.

Conflict occurs every day, and it is necessary for children to learn to sort out difficulties with others. Arguments over who owns the pencil or who cut in line are perfect examples. Name-calling and teasing may be bullying behavior; however, it depends on the context. If children have equal status in a friendship, this can be part of normal horseplay. For children who are unequal in status (for example, an older student with a kindergartner or a group of children teasing a solitary child) the same

## A CLASSROOM SNAPSHOT . . .

*As I learned about the characteristics of bullies, I began to link these profiles to students I had in my classroom.*

### CHAD

Chad had been an ongoing concern at my school since first grade. He had always been much smaller in stature than his classmates, but what he lacked in size he more than made up for in attitude. He displayed little interest in or empathy for others' feelings, and seemed to take special delight in taunting children until they cried. A very bright boy, Chad did excellent work academically, but in social situations or during unstructured times he was aggressive, manipulative, and argumentative.

While most children tried to avoid Chad, several boys hung out with him and often took part when he bullied others, possibly to avoid becoming targets themselves.

Chad was the baby of his family and seemed to rule his parents quite effectively. His parents appeared unconcerned about the situation, and implied that it was the school's fault and the school's problem.

### CLAIRE

Claire, a new girl in the school, had become the center of a group of girls who were impressed by the fact she had recently moved here from California. Unfortunately, Claire ruled her group with an iron fist and was making life for some of the girls in my class miserable. While she was very polite and cooperative with me, her power over this group was awesome. Often one of the girls was in tears at recess because for some reason, she was being taunted or ostracized from the group on Claire's orders.

### SEAN

Sean was tall for his age, towering over most of the other children in the class. He had a great heart and a real curiosity about the world around him but he had recently been formally diagnosed as AD/HD, which was not a surprise to those who knew him. Sean really wanted to have friends but was very aggressive with others. He was unable to read the social cues of his peers and seemed genuinely surprised when his behavior annoyed others. He was also very emotional, crying easily or lashing out when he felt threatened, sometimes over very minor things. There were lots of complaints about Sean on the playground but his parents were more concerned with his academic achievement than his social difficulties. As I saw it, Sean's aggression and lack of skill in the social arena were impacting his self-confidence, which in turn affected his overall school performance.

behaviors are bullying.

In a conflict situation, the behavior is often "made public" and easy to spot. For example, on playground supervision days, I notice that sixth-grade boys, in particular, delight in jockeying for power. In these situations, whether they are play-fighting, teasing, or engaging in real conflict, it is obvious that the boys involved, and the children watching, all have relatively the same social status within the group; that is, they are usually friends who are matched up against each other and each boy is supported by friends. These "fights," even if serious, last briefly and usually take place in some visible spot. They tend to end if one person becomes really angry, or is hurt, and usually the boys are friendly after the fact.

CREATING A BULLY-FREE CLASSROOM

## CHARACTERISTICS OF BULLIED CHILDREN

Bullied children may:

- be vulnerable in some way. They may be isolated from their peers and not have many friends, be very shy, or be very submissive and timid. They may not read social cues effectively.

- lack confidence in themselves in social situations. They may be unsure of how to deal with others and unable to stand up for themselves effectively.

- have difficulty controlling their emotions; they may cry easily or become extremely angry very quickly.

- sometimes exhibit behaviors that are annoying to others.

- "look different" in some way (e.g., physical disability, race). However, this tends not to be the only factor; lacking friends who will stand up for them and exhibiting the characteristics mentioned above are much more crucial factors.

- simply be in the wrong place at the wrong time.

*Keep in mind that there are no acceptable reasons for children to be bullied. No one deserves to be harassed for any reason. However, these characteristics shed light on specific ways we can support bullied children, such as teaching them strategies and skills to help develop their confidence when dealing with bullies—the focus of Chapters 3, 4, and 5.*

Bullying, however, often takes place out of sight of adults and always involves aggression and intimidation. It's an abuse of power, and its targets are usually vulnerable in some way. Once, during morning recess, a child came up to me to report that a group of girls were bothering another girl in their class. It was happening around a corner from where I was standing, so I hadn't noticed anything unusual. As I rounded the corner, the girls saw me coming and quickly disbanded. I was surprised to find that the ringleader was Vera, a former student of mine who had always been polite, easy-going, and friendly. Ginny, the girl being bullied, was timid, shy, and quiet. As I talked to her, she told me that Vera had been threatening to tell people a terrible thing about her if she didn't move out of their territory. Apparently, there was an unwritten rule that this area belonged to the "gang" and Ginny had unwittingly strayed into their space. She didn't know what terrible things they would say but was upset nonetheless. She stuck close to me the rest of recess. Later, after a discussion with Vera, her followers, and Ginny (with me doing most of the talking), they made a reluctant apology to her. It wasn't enough; I knew that more needed to be done to support children like Ginny.

## Bystanders and the Bullied Child

Bullies need quiet, "under the radar screen" areas to torment others, but more important, they rely upon either the acceptance of other children or their reluctance to become involved. These groups of children, called bystanders, are students who are on the fringe of the bullying event. They may join in with the bully or may stand silently, unwilling or unsure of how to help.

Creating a Bully-Free Classroom • Scholastic Teaching Resources

A Secret Service report indicates "that in [one-half] of the school homicides examined, the attacker told someone about the planned attack, and in nearly all cases that person was a peer—a friend, school-mate, or a sibling. They almost never told an adult" (Caldwell, 2004). Bystanders can diffuse the situation if they have the skills and awareness of how to step in or get help.

And then there are the children who are bullied. These children tend to be vulnerable in some way, and it is often tempting for adults to frame the child as a victim because of his or her perceived weakness. However, children can be targeted for many reasons and can be helped more effec-tively when we identify common characteristics of children who are hurt by bullying rather than label them with stereotypes.

## WHAT ROLE SHOULD ADULTS PLAY IN BULLYING SITUATIONS?

As I learned more about bullied children, it became obvious that I had certainly not done much to help Ben, Chad's victim. While I didn't ignore the situation, I hadn't given Ben much to work with, either. Telling him to avoid Chad was a standard piece of advice I handed out but it was inef-fective and made Ben feel even more powerless when he was unable to escape Chad's attention.

How do adults fit into the picture? Ignoring the situation isn't the answer but neither is always stepping in and resolving the problem. I discovered that setting consequences in place for children who bully helped me handle the situation temporarily, but took power away from the students themselves. In the role of "solver" I taught children very little about handling the problem and developing the confidence they would need to stand up for themselves. When should I step in and when should I step back? After all, asking students to rely on an adult to come to the rescue may work at recess but it is a pretty useless strategy in a back alley on the way home from school.

## A Road-Map to Success: The "Big Four" Plan

As I worked through my research and began to develop an action plan, I realized that bully-proofing was not a one-shot deal. Like peeling an onion, I revealed layers of challenges I would need to tackle to deal with this problem effectively. My main goal was to support bullied children, but at the same time I also wanted to help children who bullied.

I identified the needs of bullied children: bullied children need specific, nuts-and-bolts strategies to use when targeted by a bully— to stand up for themselves in positive ways, feel confident about their abilities, and insist on being treated well.

On the other hand, bullies must be shown that there are benefits to

## A STAFF-ROOM SNAPSHOT . . .

A conversation in my staff room revealed many different viewpoints about how to handle bullies. Almost everyone had at least one child who was bullying others, or had children who were being picked on. Some comments included:

*"I think that we have enough to deal with already. Just shoot 'em down to see the principal, that's what I do."*

*"I try to ignore it if no one is being hurt. After all, what else can I really do? Half the time it happens outside of school anyway. We can't be expected to walk these kids to and from home, right?"*

*"Just tell the victims to punch back. I guarantee that will solve the problem."*

*"It's a part of growing up. They have to learn to deal with it."*

*"In the real world, you've got to stand up for yourself. Fight back. Hit them hard. It worked for me."*

*"Well, I'm sorry to say that some of these kids ask for it! I mean, they don't stand up for themselves, or they cry. If they don't have a backbone, well, then, it's not surprising they're picked on."*

The more we talked about bullying (and the topic kept coming up over and over again), the more I heard the underlying frustration that many of my colleagues felt. They knew that the things they did were more often than not unsuccessful, and many were at the point where they just didn't know what to do next.

One teacher summed it up best when he said, "I don't think what I'm doing is all that effective, but for the life of me, I'm not sure what to do. After 20 years, you'd think I'd have some ideas, but I don't."

dealing positively with others. They need to develop respect, tolerance, and most important, empathy for others. They must also realize that there will be consistent and clear consequences for their behavior.

The framework I developed works for both bullied children and bullies and is organized into four teaching units that can be revisited though the year. Based in best-practice instruction for young learners, the units consist of a wide variety of approaches and materials, including children's literature, role-playing, writing, art, and movement. An outline of the program goals follows.

### Unit 1: NO MORE BULLIES/YOU HAVE THE POWER!

**Part 1**

• Establish classroom management goals beginning with standards of behavior.

• Introduce the goal of bully-proofing our classroom.

• Introduce related vocabulary to use throughout the year.

• Discuss what bullying is, how it's different from conflict, consequences for bullying, and how, by working together, we can help end bullying in our classroom and school.

Part 2

- Teach to students' personal strengths in order to help them build confidence.

- Have students create their own personal action plan and other practical tools for countering bullying behaviors.

## Unit 2: MARVELOUS ME!

- Conduct activities to develop each student's self-esteem, to reduce their vulnerability in general and to bullies in particular.

- Focus on celebrating each child's uniqueness, while allowing children to see their similarities to others.

- Help all children develop empathy and an understanding that others have interesting and valuable things to offer.

## Unit 3: FABULOUS FRIENDS

- Teach strategies for making and keeping friends.

- Help students develop empathy for other people's feelings and experiences.

## Unit 4: CONFLICT RESOLUTION

- Introduce conflict-resolution techniques.

- Teach a structured, three-step problem-solving process during arguments.

- Have students practice conflict resolution consistently in the classroom and on the playground.

By focusing on the Big Four throughout the year, we can help students develop a toolbox of strategies to use when dealing with bullies. At the same time, we can help them learn to empathize with others and acquire the confidence and skills they need to solve conflicts with others successfully.

While it may be tempting to jump in right away with quick-fix solutions for bullying in your classroom, give yourself time to design a successful course of action. Following the ideas and suggestions in Chapter 2, you'll carefully set goals and establish classroom management strategies to ensure that your plan is well designed and effective.

**CHAPTER 2**

# Launching Your Bully-Proofing Plan

*This chapter prepares you to launch your bully-proofing plan: it helps you evaluate your current approaches and beliefs, take stock of your time and resources, and trouble-shoot.*

I once taught with a wonderful principal who practiced what he preached about treating staff and students with respect and kindness. He was respected and loved in return.

One day during a staff meeting, he suddenly rounded on a colleague and began to harangue her about paying attention. On and on he went, sarcastically commenting on her lack of interest, her intelligence—the rest of us were horrified! This was entirely out of character for Don, and we couldn't believe our ears.

Suddenly, he turned to us. After taking a sip of coffee, he smiled at the victim of his wrath and thanked her. She smiled back. Mystified, we looked at each other.

"How did it feel to see me treat Sheila like that?" he asked. "How do you think it felt to be talked to like that in front of all of you?" he went on, looking at each one of us in turn.

"You were horrified by my taking Sheila to task because adults don't expect to be treated like that. Well, the students in this school shouldn't expect to, either. I'm not singling any of you out, but I've been unhappy to overhear some teachers in their classrooms talking to students disrespectfully. Children deserve to be treated with the same respect as adults do. It's easy to forget that when you're angry or frustrated. On my staff, you must always keep the dignity of the student of the utmost importance."

This episode impressed upon me the importance of mutual respect, and I have made sure this philosophy is built into the structure of the bully-proofing plan itself. If we expect bullies to treat others with respect, they need to see figures of authority in the school acting the same way. Each child, bullied, bully, or bystander, deserves to be treated with kindness and respect at all times.

The following questions guide the discussion of this chapter. Answering them as you read will help you develop the framework you'll need to build and maintain an effective bully-proofing plan.

- How do you interact with students? Do you think that most students feel positively after speaking with you, even after being disciplined? Are there things you could do to approach problem situations differently?

- Examine your personal beliefs about bullying. What experiences do you have that may affect your thinking today?

- Take a look at what you do now. What works? What doesn't work?

- What resources can you pull together to help you plan your activities and classroom organization?

- How will you implement these four components in your classroom on a daily basis? Weekly? Yearlong?

• How will your physical space affect your activities?

• What classroom management strategies will you implement to support your goals?

• What will your basic, non-negotiable classroom behavior standards be? How will you communicate these effectively to your students?

• What will your personal action plan look like?

• How will you effectively communicate your plan to parents?

## Reflecting on Your Interaction With Students

As the opening anecdote illustrates, children (and adults) who are treated disrespectfully cannot be expected to turn around and treat others properly. It is easy to forget that, as teachers, we model all types of behavior unknowingly every day in our classrooms and beyond, so it becomes essential for each of us to realize the behaviors we demonstrate color the tone and effectiveness of the message we are trying to convey to our students.

Sarcasm, public discipline, and put-downs can devastate a child. Many adults remember a teacher who publicly humiliated them by making fun of them in front of others. Treatment like this diminishes both the child's dignity and the respect children have for the teacher.

We have to be sure that our words are in line with our practice. It can be very difficult, when dealing with a child who has repeatedly bullied others, to remember that all children need to be treated with dignity and respect. Teachers are human beings, and we become frustrated and angry. In the heat of the moment, it's easy to speak before we think. But if we expect our students to speak to others respectfully and deal with problems privately, then we have to ensure that we do the same. It is part of our responsibility to treat all of our students the same way, even when it is most challenging!

List your best approaches to handling students with care and respect and take some time to envision new approaches where a kinder hand is needed. Are there other ways to model respectful behaviors (e.g., through role-playing a friendly disagreement with a colleague or inviting older students to model a respectful conversation with peers)?

*How do you interact with students? Do you think that most students feel positively after speaking with you, even after being disciplined? Are there things you could do to approach problem situations differently?*

## Examining Your Personal Beliefs About Bullying

Many of us have been bullies and have been bullied. Where does this lead our thinking as adults and teachers? Consider how your personal beliefs about bullying affect what you do in your classroom today.

When I began to think about my attitudes towards bullies and

*What experiences do you have that may affect your thinking today?*

**CHAPTER 2**

bullying, episodes in my own life came back to me. I remembered seventh grade when I was new to the school, had few friends, and weighed 98 pounds soaking wet! Frequently, I was the target of bullies and I clearly remember the fear and helplessness I felt. My tactics for survival included avoiding my tormentors, trying to blend in with the furniture, and "going along" with the teasing. I chose not to tell anyone about what was happening because I was embarrassed and fearful of even worse treatment. So why would I be surprised or frustrated that kids were reluctant to seek help when I had felt the same way? The strategies I now offered bullied children were simply variations on tactics I had tried myself in seventh grade, which were neither helpful nor successful.

> Many children experiment with intimidating someone else but stop when confronted with their behavior. This common experience may be where the myth that bullying is a part of growing up originates. However, whether it occurs as a one-time incident or a repeated pattern of behavior, bullying must be dealt with.

While dealing with bullies, I also felt frustrated. My memory of a junior high school bullying incident in which a group of peers and I had picked on another girl reminded me that bullying fulfilled a need to feel powerful; however, I wasn't sure how to successfully deal with that, either.

This would be a good time to go back and use the Bullying: True or False? statements in Chapter 1 to guide your thinking. What statements did you accept as fact? How do you think your beliefs have been shaped by your experiences? You may choose to write down your revelations and thoughts based upon this reflection; these may be helpful to you as you plan your strategies and management techniques or to refresh your thinking if you begin to feel off-track during the year.

*What resources can you pull together to help you plan your activities and classroom organization?*

## Collecting Resources

As you gather resources, help yourself stay organized by creating a place to store your ideas and plans. The bully-proofing resource book described below can be used year after year to help you plan and share your ideas with colleagues, administrators, and parents.

### CREATING A BULLY-PROOFING RESOURCE BOOK

Your resource book will be the place you store information, lessons, and ideas that you come across during the year and can help you implement the ideas discussed in upcoming chapters. Include copies of successful lesson plans, copies of work sheets, lists of books and videos, and other materials you can use throughout the year. You may also want to store anecdotal records involving your students here.

**Resource books may include:**

- your list of bully-proofing strategies that work

- a list of books, videos, or DVD's on bullying that you have either used or want to use with your students (This could include a photocopy of the annotated bibliography in the appendix.)

- photocopied pages of professional books (Highlight information you find especially helpful and ideas you want to try.)

- clear pocket pages (or sticky photo-album pages) to store articles and newspaper clippings

- a copy of any materials you use (transparencies, work sheets, and so on)

- copies of letters, newsletters, and so on that you've sent home.

- a floppy disc or CD-ROM containing any of the materials you've created (This can be stored in a clear pocket page or resealable bag with holes punched into one side.)

- anecdotal records, or a bullying log regarding any bullying incidents involving your students

Your reflection on your beliefs and attitudes will become the first page of the resource book. Encourage yourself to reflect back honestly and note changes in your perceptions as you implement your plan.

> **WHICH FORMAT WILL WORK FOR YOU?**
> Resource books can take many forms, but I've found a binder to be the easiest to use. You can quickly and easily add new information and organize materials so they are at your fingertips.

## Taking Stock—Strategies That Work

Take a look at your current strategies. Do you have a plan for dealing with bullying situations or do you just respond the best you can at the time?

*Take a look at what you do now. What works? What doesn't work?*

Is there anything that you do to prevent or deal with bullying situations that is successful? For example, I've found that having a bully make a written apology to a bullied child is more meaningful than a verbal apology, and it sometimes enables me to help the bully examine his or her behavior and how it affected another person.

List all of the strategies you currently use that work when you help students deal with bullying situations. As you come across new ideas, add them to this list, which will give you an excellent resource to use when you are desperate. Add these strategies to your resource book.

At this point, it's appropriate to consider how you could organize your time and, to a lesser degree, your physical space.

*How will you implement your program on a daily basis? Weekly? Yearlong?*

## Implementing the "Big Four"

To ensure that your plan works, the Big Four areas—building an awareness of bullying, nurturing students' self-confidence, fostering friendships, and teaching conflict resolution skills—must become an integral part of everyday life in your classroom.

While talking about bullying may occur naturally as events take place throughout the school day, it's very important to realize you can't deal with these issues on a sporadic basis. You must build in regular times for bully-proofing in your class—it's too easy to let other things crowd it out!

First, look at your plan for the year. Decide when you will begin each unit. Will you block in class discussion time or Show and Tell sessions every week? (Chapter 5 contains ideas for Show and Tell variations and other esteem-building activities.) Are there important school events like heritage celebrations that might tie in with self-esteem building and fostering friendships? When you plan school assemblies, how can you use students' experiences to reinforce key concepts about bully-proofing and community?

Looking at your daily schedule, match your students' energy with your program objectives. I found that a 15-minute session right after quiet reading was a great time to have class meetings or bullying discussions, because everyone was settled and relaxed.

Each of the Big Four units outlined in Chapters 3 to 7 will take four to six weeks to complete, and weekly follow-up discussions or activities will continue throughout your school year. This does take time, but it's time well spent.

When planning class meetings, keep sessions short; it's always better to have three or four fifteen-minute chunks than a one-hour session, unless the follow-up activities you choose take more time. Use a blank day-plan (or week-plan) and begin to consider where you could block out the short periods of time you will need. (If you need to classify this time, many activities may closely relate to language arts and health.)

Add these plans to your resource book.

*How will your physical space affect your activities?*

## Making Classroom Space Work for You

If your school permits you to organize your classroom furniture, think seriously about the physical space you have to work with. By arranging desks in groups or pushing them into a circle, you create a large space that allows for group discussions. (If maintaining student privacy while working is an issue, create "mini-offices" by taping decorated file folders around desk edges.)

Make the meeting area a comfortable, welcoming place to gather. In the meeting area in my classroom, I brought in a small carpet and as a class we created small pillows for everyone to use. My class decorated an old washing machine carton and added a door. This "reading house" and a very inexpensive children's pup tent, were available for quiet conversations. (Be sure you can fit inside, too!)

Grouping desks also creates room for a "private" area for children to meet and resolve issues. Folding cardboard display boards (or trifolds) are often used for displays and are available in office supply stores. These are terrific—cheap, effective, and lightweight, and they can be set up in seconds and taken down just as easily. They are tall enough to provide privacy but short enough for you to keep an eye on the rest of the students. These "walls" can also double as bulletin board space.

Now that you've considered the "nuts-and-bolts," practical issues of organizing your time and space, it's appropriate to move on to the framework of classroom management strategies that will help support your classroom ethic: How will you expect your students to behave and treat others? How will you communicate this clearly to students and parents?

## Classroom Management

Children must learn to make good decisions about themselves and their behavior. The only way to do this is to allow them to make decisions! While you are the adult and will need to make some decisions about how things are done, there are many ways that students can have input into the routines or expectations of your room.

Ask for students' ideas to solve a problem:

*What classroom management strategies will you implement to support your goals?*

*"We are having a traffic jam when everyone tries to put their spelling notebooks in the basket; what can we do about this?" "Everyone rushes to be the first in line when we go to the gym. Does anyone have an idea for a fair way to fix this?"*

### Voting is great way to introduce students to participating in a democracy

—everyone has a say in the decision. I usually take a "secret" vote. Sometimes, I have students put both hands over their eyes and then stick their tongue out as their vote. (Rude, yes, but it's fun, easy to count, and prevents children from peeking and being influenced or upset by the way their peers are voting.) I also use a quick secret ballot (scrap paper on which children write "Y" or "N," or "Choice 1" or "Choice 2") and then count them in front of the class.

I also don't allow groaning or complaining when a result is announced. A decision has been reached fair and square. While it's fine to disagree with the result, it is not acceptable to behave in a way that may make others feel bad that they voted the "wrong" way. A decision has been reached and it's time to move on.

**CHAPTER 2**

Issues like this can be resolved during a class meeting. However, there are times when either there are too many ideas (and some students become upset when their idea is not chosen) or the issue is a difficult one. A strategy I use is to have students write out their ideas and submit them. I choose the two or three most suitable responses and then have the class decide from those. This way I have some control over the outcome but students still feel they have the power to make their classroom a better place.

Suggestion boxes are another way to encourage students to give you some feedback on classroom issues. Consider inviting students to write a monthly letter to you about how things are going in the classroom and then responding to the letters. Time-consuming, yes, but it's amazing how much students will tell you if they know that you will treat their comments seriously, confidentially, and appreciatively. In short, they will feel that you are a friend who will really listen to their views and concerns.

*What will your basic, non-negotiable class-room behavior standards be? How will you communicate these effectively to your students?*

## Developing Your Basic, Non-Negotiable Behavior Standards

One common pitfall for new classroom managers is the assumption that students know and understand the basic rules of a classroom. Unfortunately, these assumptions and reality are often far apart! From time to time, even veteran teachers need to remind themselves of the behavior standards they have set and why these standards are so important. Keep in mind that children need to be taught and need to understand the "why's" of standards and rules, even if these seem self-evident to you.

Your standards should be non-negotiable and pretty well cover most situations that come up in the classroom. Make sure that they are aligned with your school's policies regarding behavior.

In my classroom, I introduce the **standards of behavior** that I expect the children to follow on the very first day of school each year:

**Treat everyone with respect.**

**Don't do anything to others that you wouldn't want done to you.**

**Everyone must feel safe in our classroom.**

In the early grades the three standards highlighted in the box at left are enough to begin with; others can be added during the year. Plan to spend the first few days discussing each one and listing the kinds of behavior that you expect to see for each. To reinforce these ideas, I have students create something tangible to remind them of our standards. One year, the children drew pictures (and I wrote the words backward in fabric crayon) on plain white fabric to create pillows that were then used for group time. Another year, we created T-shirts with these slogans and then wore them on special days.

When you are ready, begin to add and discuss specific classroom rules about behavior, including consequences.

## A CLASSROOM SNAPSHOT . . .

Here's a sample of the rules that my first and second graders felt were important for the class to follow:

No stealing. People like to keep their things. If you steal, you must replace what you took and say you are sorry. Then you have to tell your parents.

Taking pencils that are on the floor is not stealing. Put your stuff away and it won't be a problem.

No "budging" in line. No keeping a space in line for friends. If you do this, you have to go to the end of the line for one whole day.

(Five to seven rules is a manageable number for the younger grades.) These rules should ideally come from the students; it's so important for children to feel they have some power and control in making decisions about how their classroom will run. Take the time to link the rules children create to the standards you have established (e.g., "Let the speaker finish before you take a turn" might fall under the standard "Treat everyone with respect"). This discussion helps children understand the "why's" and realize that rules aren't arbitrary.

These rules should be posted in a conspicuous place and should be illustrated by the children. When my classes need a little extra reminding, I tape a copy of the rules list onto everyone's desk top (including mine!). These rules are also sent home to parents in our weekly newsletter. (See page 29 for ideas on how to set up an effective weekly newsletter.)

## Creating a Personal Action Plan

So far you have put a lot of thought into the structure and tone of your classroom. Now it's time to think about the steps you will take when a bullying situation arises. Of course every situation is unique, but having a plan places you firmly in control when you must deal with the bully and the bullied child. Take a few minutes to read the sample plan below and develop your own working outline, keeping in mind that the rest of this book will help you fine-tune your plan. This will be your personal action plan (your students will create one for themselves during the first unit). Be sure to add your plan to your resource book.

*What will your personal action plan look like?*

## My Action Plan: Grades 1 and 2

1. **Conduct face-to-face meetings with each party involved:** bullied child first, then bully, then bystanders.

   a. Have younger students tell their story out loud; have older students write their version of what happened.

2. **Conduct group meeting:** all parties meet and discuss, using conflict resolution format (see Chapter 7).

**PLAN A**  **FIRST-TIME PROBLEM:**

1. **Respond to the bully**.

   a. Ask for a written apology.

   b. Oversee restitution.

2. **Respond to the bullied student.**

   a. Set up discreet follow-up discussion (daily for a week).

   b. Contact the student's parents.

3. **Respond to the bystanders.**

   a. Follow up if appropriate.

4. **Add incident to anecdotal records.**

**PLAN B**  **SECOND BULLYING PROBLEM AND/OR BULLY IS UNRESPONSIVE**

1. **Respond to the bully**.

   a. Ask for a written apology.

   b. Use strategies from resource book. (e.g., Have students miss recess or another meaningful non-curriculum activity in order to write a plan for appropriate behavior. Must be supervised.)

   c. Call the student's parents.

2. **Add report to anecdotal records.**

**PLAN C**  **CONTINUED BULLYING BY STUDENT** (same target, other targets):

1. **Meet with principal.**

   a. Set up support program for bully (see Chapter 8).

2. **Meet with parents, principal, and bully.**

   a. Develop a plan of consequences for home and school.

3. **Respond to the repeatedly-bullied child (if applicable).**

   a. Schedule follow-up meetings.

   • Review personal action plan, and add new strategies.

   • Monitor daily through oral or written communication (e.g., folded note in shoe: "How's it going?").

   b. Call parents; set up meeting if appropriate.

4. **Respond to the bystanders:**

   a. Schedule follow-up discussions.

   • Review personal action plan; have them answer: *What will I do next time?*

Think about what you will do first. Holding face-to-face discussions with the children involved is fundamental to any plan. Will you meet with the students together or individually to hear about the problem? Will you include bystanders at this point? This may depend on the particular children you're dealing with. If you're working with older children, you may have them write out a statement of events first.

According to my sample plan, I meet with each child involved first, then any bystanders. Finally, I bring the main participants together. I proceed in this way for two reasons: first, I can hear both sides privately and ask any questions I need to in a calmer setting; second, it gives me time to think about my approach.

First-time problems are usually relatively simple to resolve. The bully should be sincere in his or her apology and willing to make restitution if possible. Damage to personal property, stealing lunches, and so on, may be relatively easy to fix. Other forms of bullying may require a personal pledge; that is, the bully must be specific about how he or she will behave the next time. Having students use "I" statements in which they are the subject (for example, *I was wrong* rather than *It was wrong*) helps hold students accountable for their actions and "own" their pledge. Older children can write down their pledge and each child involved can sign it. Alert parents with a phone call and send home copies. Keep another copy in the student's files.

> Restitution means "fixing what you did." *Barbara Coloroso (2003)*

If this is a repeated problem and the bully is not honoring his or her pledge, then Plan B would go into effect, providing a much more comprehensive framework to follow.

Each time you work through your personal action plan, keep tabs on the specific steps you take in your anecdotal record book. These notes enable you to track and identify patterns of student behavior, and provide you with an invaluable resource when talking to parents or administrators.

## KEEPING EFFECTIVE ANECDOTAL RECORDS

No matter the format, anecdotal records must be comprehensive but easy to maintain. Effective records include a date, names of all involved, a brief summary of the problem, the consequences and the follow-up. Here are a few ideas:

• Create and copy your own form or make copies of the Bullying Incident Report reproducible on page 106. Keep several blank copies in your plan-book for easy access, and then add each completed form to your resource book.

• Assign one page of your resource book to each child. When a child is involved in an incident, jot it down on a sticky note and stick it to the front cover of your Resource book. Then, when you have time, affix the note to the child's page. If more than one student is involved, photocopy the note and staple the copies into the book. Alternately, use a clipboard with a stack of legal-size paper. Create a grid with enough room to write down information about each bullying problem. When it is full, cut it apart and staple onto each child's page in your resource book. Make copies of notes if necessary.

• Use a student notebook. Write the date of the incident in the margin as well as the names of the students involved before using point-form notes to detail the problem. I sometimes highlight the dates and names to enable me to find information more easily.

Whichever method you choose, make sure that these records are kept in a secure area. Respecting students' privacy is very important.

Following the entire plan does take time, but because you've thought out the process, it becomes easier to both make the time to deal with problems as they occur and to decide upon the course of action to take. The more you use your plan, the faster and easier it will be to resolve these issues and move onto the rest of the day.

*How will you communicate your plan to parents?*

## Making the Home–School Connection

As indicated in the sample plan, another important part of bully-proofing is clear and consistent communication with parents. In your daily plan, make sure to set a regular time to contact parents about these issues. One of the biggest complaints that parents have is not being aware their child has been involved in bullying situations.

*One of the biggest complaints that parents have is not being aware their child has been involved in bullying situations.*

With a record of every incident (see the previous section), you can show parents patterns of behavior. One benefit of keeping parents involved from the beginning, is that since they know their child best, they often have valuable input as to appropriate consequences. I prefer to phone parents, if possible, because I gain so much more information from speaking to them.

If a parent is not supportive or concerned about a bullying issue, inform your administrator as soon as possible. Sometimes parents won't take bullying seriously until your principal is involved.

Parents have a right to be informed about your classroom and school policies, and so the final area to consider is how you will communicate this to parents on a regular, comprehensive basis. Parent nights are a terrific way to discuss with parents your basic behavior expectations, and explain your bullying plan. Parents need to be aware of the steps you will take if children are involved in bullying incidents, and when you spell out

## A CLASSROOM SNAPSHOT . . .

A successful way to communicate with parents is to send home a weekly classroom newsletter.

One basic routine in my classroom is scheduled for the last ten minutes each day: as a class we brainstorm and list the things we have accomplished that day in class. I make sure I add information about our discussion topics, such as bully-proofing. We also include exciting news, like who lost a tooth or who had a birthday, which seems to increase the chances of the newsletter actually making it home!

If you are lucky enough to have a computer in your classroom, create a newsletter template and then type in your sentences each day as the children suggest them. Otherwise, use a large sheet of chart paper, or even a special space on your blackboard to write. (Use it as an opportunity to model writing skills.)

On Fridays at noon, print out the newsletter, make copies, and have it ready to send home at the end of the day. (This is a terrific activity for volunteers to take on.) If there's time, give the students a chance to decorate it.

The newsletter is both a convenient way to keep parents informed and a constant reminder that you consider them partners in their child's education. Over the years, I've received many, many comments from parents who appreciated knowing what activities and topics of discussion we were covering.

the specific actions you will take, it reassures parents that all children will be treated fairly and consistently and that no child is being "singled out" or being picked on.

● ● ●

Now you have carefully considered key questions that will help you design and launch an effective long-term plan. You've drafted a personal action plan, and you have your materials and procedures in a handy resource book. You have made important decisions about how you will communicate your behavior expectations to students and parents. Your road map is in place and it's time to navigate the first part of your plan: addressing bullying directly with students and teaching them strategies to eliminate bullying in your classroom.

# No More Bullies!

## *(The Big Four, Unit One—Part One)*

*This chapter presents the first half of unit one with lessons and activities that help you introduce classroom goals for bully-proofing, set ground rules for group discussions, and teach basic concepts about bullying.*

Chad was at it again. Ben came into the classroom a few days later with a tear-stained face and his shirt askew. I quietly pulled him aside and heard a now familiar tale. Chad had chased him, pulled on the back of his shirt, and then stolen his recess snack.

Ben and I talked about what had happened. I reassured him that the bullying he was experiencing was not his fault and that I knew he and other children in the class were having trouble with bullies. We were going to do something about it. With that, I pulled out my personal action plan and showed Ben the steps we would go through to try and resolve this problem. Once he could see that I was going to do something, he looked quite hopeful.

Next, I met with Chad during library time and got his side of the story. As I expected, he felt Ben had provoked him because he had run away when Chad had "just gone over to see what he had for a recess snack."

Interestingly, when I asked Chad to tell me what a bully was, he couldn't seem to link his own behavior with the examples of bullying he gave me. Bullies, to him, were always older children who kicked you and made fun of you. He was quite taken aback when he heard the definition of a bully. When I showed him my personal action plan, he began to realize that I was going to hold him accountable for his behavior and there were going to be consequences for him.

Following my plan, I had Chad and Ben write a brief version of what had happened. When the two boys came together, I asked Ben to read his description first. While the boys disagreed on many points, there were similarities in both versions and Chad grudgingly admitted that, yes, some of the things Ben said were true and he had "forgotten" to write those parts down. Ben had the opportunity to describe to Chad how he felt when he was being harassed and told him what he wanted Chad to do the next time they were outside at recess.

"Chad," Ben said, "you always take my recess snack and that really hurts my feelings and it makes me mad, too. If you just ask me, maybe I'll give you some, unless it's my favorite."

Chad looked thoughtful. After both boys had said everything they felt they needed to say, I sent Chad off to think about an apology. I introduced the idea of restitution and wondered out loud how he could fix what he had done.

After school that day, Chad delivered an apology note that was decorated with some small pictures showing Ben giving Chad some of his snack. As restitution, and without any prompting, Chad suggested that he bring a snack for Ben the next day. And he did.

While things had worked out this time, I didn't believe for a moment that Chad had reformed; it was, however, a successful first step.

The thing that really struck me about Chad's reaction was his lack of awareness about bullying. I wondered how many other children were unsure of what bullying really was. Therefore, defining bullying—giving children the vocabulary they would need—and encouraging children to work together to deal with this issue became the focus of the first part of my bully-proofing work in the classroom.

No More Bullies! the first part of the bully-proofing unit, is organized in five steps:

1. Introducing the Bully-Proofing Unit and Group Discussion Rules

2. Defining Bullying and Sharing Experiences

3. Helping Students Understand the Difference Between Bullying and Conflict

4. Creating Closure: Consequences and Apologies

5. Working Together to End Bullying

# 1 Introducing the Bully-Proofing Unit and Group Discussion Rules

Begin by gathering your students in a group and telling them about the bully-proofing activities you will work on together for the next few weeks and throughout the year. Talk about the fact that you have noticed bullying in your classroom and school.

Underscore the point that bullying makes a school and a classroom feel unsafe, and that doesn't mesh with your **standards of behavior.** Here are the three basic rules I spell out for students at the beginning of the year:

• Treat everyone with respect.

• Don't do anything to others you wouldn't want done to you.

• Everyone must feel safe in our classroom. (See Chapter 2 for more on how to set up these behavior standards.)

You can assure students, "By learning how to deal with people who are bullies and by looking out for each other, we will make people feel safe and happy to be here."

Begin by discussing the rules of class meetings. Many activities in this unit are based on group discussions so setting ground rules for behavior during discussions or circle meetings with your class is important. These rules should be firmly set and non-negotiable. To successfully focus the direction of discussions, be prepared to begin your sessions with a clearly stated goal.

> *"Today, we're going to talk about how to help someone who is being bullied."*

Opening up the floor to general discussions about bullying tends to bog down the conversation and students easily veer off topic. Be prepared to steer the conversation back to the topic at hand. If you sense that there is interest in a certain area, such as playground monitor responsibilities, note it and return to it another time. This way, you prevent the discussions from going places you are not comfortable or

**NOTE:**
Please use the suggested lesson and activity ideas as guidelines and modify the ideas to meet the needs of your class. The activities I describe are designed to be used in small chunks of time; however, you may want to focus on certain elements more intensively. For example, you may want to devote both discussion and activity time to the group rules for several days before you move on to the next part of the activity. Take as much (or as little) time as you need. You know your students, and you know what will work best in your classroom.

**CHAPTER 3**

ready to deal with. Bullying issues can be very emotional for children.

Create a chart listing the discussion rules you will use during class time and post it in a prominent spot. Write the rules on chart paper, using a new color for each rule. Different colors allow younger children to find a rule quickly.

 *"Ben, can you please read the blue rule for us?"*
*"Sherry, please remember the orange rule."*

## DISCUSSION RULES FOR OUR CLASSROOM

**We never allow names to be used in bullying discussions.** If you are telling us about a time you were bullied, you must call the bully "Person X." (This rule ensures that children will not be put on the spot for real or imagined events, and it means that all children will be treated respectfully. I've found that students enjoy this rule because it appeals to their imagination and sense of fair play.)

**One person at a time may speak.** Everyone has the right to speak without being interrupted. (I've used a beanbag or a ball for this. The person holding the ball is the only person who may speak.)

**Problems between people need to be solved at a different time.** Bring up problems with a classmate at the right time. (Often, children bring up arguments with others during these discussions. Remind them to use their conflict-resolution problem-solving skills at a more appropriate time. See Chapter 7 for ways to make conflict resolution a successful part of your bully-free plan)

**No put-downs, silly comments, or laughter when others are talking.** Respect each speaker—everyone has something valuable to add.

Children must understand the reasons why these are rules to be followed. If you link them back to the ground rules of your classroom, it should be obvious to your students that you will make sure every child is treated with respect and dignity. Because these rules are so important, it is worthwhile to take some time to help children remember them. Read them aloud frequently and encourage children to repeat the rules often. Have the class chant them with you or read each rule with a different sound—use a monster voice! a teeny-tiny voice! a squeaky voice! Sing it, whisper it, roar it. You might even have a student play "teacher" and point to the words as everyone reads. One of my students' favorite activities is listening to me read the rules and catching me as I deliberately make mistakes—"We must *always* say the person's real name." Children love catching adults' mistakes—the sillier the mistake the better.

To extend this activity for younger children, make copies of the rules for each child. Invite children to be "word detectives," finding basic reading words (*we, to, in, at* . . .) and circling them. You might also use sticky notes to cover words on the chart paper and challenge children to fill in the correct word, using context clue skills. Have older students copy the rules in cursive writing.

## 2 Defining Bullying and Sharing Experiences

Lizi Boyd's *Bailey the Big Bully* offers a great way to initiate a discussion about bullies. In the story, Bailey torments others in his class until Max arrives and stands up to Bailey. Although the adults provide little support

**Literature Link:**

*Bailey the Big Bully*
by Lizi Boyd
(Penguin, 1989)

and Max resorts to punching Bailey (an act for which he is disciplined), the story also demonstrates appropriate ways of dealing with bullies. Max and his friends show Bailey ways to be a friend, and reach out to include him in their activities. The story is resolved in a positive way.

After reading the book, ask the students how they knew Bailey was a bully. Begin a list of the behaviors that can be classified as bullying. On the top of your chart paper, list the four main types of bullying: physical, social (bullying within friendships, such as exclusion), verbal (put-downs, taunts, name-calling, starting rumors), and intimidation (threats, making someone do something, extortion). You may need to change the language so it's age appropriate (for example, "words that hurt" for "verbal bullying").

Discuss each type, and have students give an example from the book. As you add behaviors to the list, you may need to steer the discussion and include behaviors that were not mentioned in the book. Is teasing a way to bully someone? What about laughing at someone? At this point, introduce the definition of a bully.

> A bully is a person who threatens, scares, or hurts other people so they will do what the bully wants.

It's important not to focus much attention on why people are bullies. As noted in Chapter 1, there are many reasons, and a discussion about these may put a child who is a bully in a vulnerable position. Respecting all children's rights to privacy and feeling safe must be paramount in these discussions.

By the same token, be careful about the emphasis placed on the

**CHAPTER 3**

actual examples of bullying. While you should talk about the four main types of bullying and refer often to the chart you created, focusing intensely on specific things that cause pain to others can backfire. (You don't want a bully to pick up any new material from your discussion!)

By now, most if not all of your students will want to share stories about times they were bullied. Take advantage of this enthusiasm, and have each child draw and/or write about a time he or she was bullied. You may need to write younger children's sentences on the bottom of their pictures. Be sure to remind children of the "no names" rule.

Explain that these pages will be collected and turned into a new class book. This often encourages children to put more time and effort into their work. As well, it is an easy and effective way for each child to share his or her story in a controlled way; it takes far less time than allowing everyone to share a story orally, and it prevents awkward situations—if one child has

## Easy Ways to Create Class Books

**A few simple ways to create a class book:**

- For a sturdy temporary book, staple all the pages together at the top and attach the booklet to a clipboard. (The clip will fit right along the stapled binding so pages can be turned as students hold the board.) Tape the last page on the board to keep the book in place.

- Punch a hole at the top corner of the pages and use a binder ring to hold the booklet together. This makes a quick book, but one that lacks durability, which may or may not be a concern. (Some class books are only meant to be used for a short time.) Stapling books, or putting them into a binder, a duo-tang, or plastic report covers helps books last longer. To add strength and prevent pages from tearing out, put a strip of clear tape along the

hole-punched edge before you punch or staple. You may also want to laminate the front and back covers for durability.

- Use file folders to create book covers. Punch two holes through a closed folder, put the pages inside and use a long steel prong (available at office supply stores), wool, or binder rings to fasten.

- Bind the pages with a coil-binding machine—this binding makes a sturdy, good-looking class book.

- If there will be fewer than 20 pages and you have access to a sewing machine, you can sew the binding. (Experiment with your machine; some can sew thicker books.) Use a straight stitch, sew up the left side (or top) of the book, and then cover with masking tape or fabric tape to hide the stitches.

**Materials tip:** Have children work on copier paper, which is more resilient than lined paper. If lines are needed, photocopy pages that have blank areas for illustrations as well as lines. To create a uniform design, you might use a computer to create borders, and then make copies for each student.

named another child, you can gently remind him or her of the "no names" rule and have the child remove the name or distinguishing feature from the work, rather than having to react to the situation after a bully or bullied child has been put in the spotlight in a group-share situation.

I share stories of times I was bullied and make sure I describe how helpless, sad, and angry I felt. (At this point, I don't get into what I did to solve the problem.) It makes a huge impression on children to realize that you understand and have had the same problems as they do. I make a big deal out of adding my page to the class book, as this is also a perfect time to model writing behaviors.

Agree on a title for the book and have each child sign the cover. Make sure it's available in the room for children to read independently.

## 3 Helping Students Understand the Difference Between Bullying and Conflict

This lesson highlights the difference between bullying behavior and normal conflict, as discussed in Chapter 1. It's important for children to understand that conflict is a normal part of daily life and can often be resolved by talking out the problem. Bullying, however, is much different. Students need to recognize the hallmarks of bullying behavior and how to get help.

Begin the next lesson by reading the class book you've created with students from the previous lesson. After reading the book, take a few moments to go over the definition of a bully. (If necessary, review the rules of classroom discussions.) Then refer students back to the list of bullying behaviors they recorded from the story of Bailey. Ask if students noticed any new behaviors described in the class book. You may choose to add them to the class list.

At this point it becomes important to begin to introduce the language you will use throughout the year. *Conflict* is a term students will become familiar with and is an easy one to teach because there are so many examples all around us!

Gather a few familiar fiction books that you and your class have read. You might also include a comic book or two, an animated movie that all students are familiar with (anything by Disney is usually a good bet), or a book based on a popular television show.

Introduce the idea that conflict is something that is around us every day. Define conflict and ask students for examples. Look at the books, comics, movies, and any other examples you have gathered and have your students agree on the conflict within each story. Older students can work with the materials in small groups, decide what the main conflict is, and then report back to the class. Use this opportunity to teach about conflict

**CHAPTER 3**

in books and cartoons and introduce story structure. All fiction has some form of conflict—which drives the plot—and a resolution.

For older children, Elizabeth Levy's *Third Grade Bullies* underscores the difference between bullying and conflict. Sally, a new girl in third grade, sees her classmate Tina being bullied. Sally helps Tina stand up for herself. In the meantime, Sally is involved in a conflict situation with a boy named Darcy and the difference between the two situations is clearly drawn.

> **Literature Link:**
> *Third Grade Bullies*
> by Elizabeth Levy
> (Hyperion, 1998)
> (for older students)

After establishing what conflict is, define for students the difference between bullying and conflict. List the main differences between conflict and bullying, using age-appropriate language. A T-chart is a good way to highlight the differences.

**WHAT'S THE DIFFERENCE BETWEEN BULLYING AND CONFLICT?**

| Bullying | Conflict |
|---|---|
| • happens in secrecy or out-of-the way places | • often happens where everyone can see what's happening |
| • someone is targeting one person | • usually has lots of people around and involved |
| • threats are used, and bullies hurt people with words or actions | • may involve fighting, but both people fight and it usually stops quickly |
| • are not friends with their targets | • afterward, usually the problem is worked out and people are friends again |

**Most important, bullying results in one person feeling that he or she is in danger.**

Take time to talk about the issue of fighting. Stress that people get angry and that's okay, but physical fighting and hurting others is not okay. Refer to *Bailey the Big Bully;* Max hit Bailey and Max was the one who got into trouble. Hitting Bailey didn't solve the problem. Talking out conflict is always the best way to go. You may want to review your school's policies on fighting with your students. (For older students, this may be an appropriate time to begin to introduce the conflict-resolution skills and strategies discussed in Chapter 7. However, if it's not practical to begin teaching children these skills at this point, flag and return to this conflict discussion when you are ready to introduce conflict resolution.)

To end this lesson (and to prepare for the next one), use the reproducible "Conflict or Bullying?" on page 37. This sheet provides a series of anecdotes describing either conflict or bullying situations. Ask children to listen carefully and either put their hand on their head if the scenario you read shows bullying or cross their arms if it shows conflict. This gives you a quick visual assessment of students' comprehension. You'll know immediately whether you are ready to move on or if you need to spend more time on the bullying/conflict concept.

# Conflict or Bullying?

*Use the following scenarios to help children identify the difference between conflict and bullying.*

Sally and Linda are sitting on the swings. Two boys come over and ask them for a turn on the swings. Sally says no, and goes on swinging. The boys are angry and start yelling at the girls, and then the boys go off to find a teacher.                                                CONFLICT

Bobby is missing his favorite pencil. He suddenly sees Jimmy using it. "Hey, give me back my pencil!" he yells. Jimmy tells him he found it on the floor and now it's his pencil. Bobby takes Jimmy's eraser and throws it into the garbage can.                                        CONFLICT

Three boys are in the boys' bathroom, and they start throwing wet paper towels all over the floor and laughing. A boy from another class comes in to wash his hands after art. The three boys start throwing wet paper towels at him, and when he tells them to stop, they threaten to go and tell his teacher he threw the towels. They tell him to pick up the mess, or else. Then one boy kicks him in the leg.        BULLYING

A group of girls in third grade have been friends since first grade. One day, Susan tells the other girls not to be friends anymore with Amy. The other girls agree and run away from Amy at recess and lunch. They won't tell her why, and she starts to cry because she doesn't know why they are doing this to her.                                        BULLYING

On the way home from school, Greg is chased by the biggest boy in his class, Steve. Steve pulls him behind a garbage can and tells Greg to bring him a recess snack tomorrow. Steve threatens Greg and tells him if he knows what's good for him, he'll do it.                        BULLYING

Billy likes to play soccer, but Jordan plays rough and Billy tries not to play when he's there. One game, Jordan tripped him during the game and Billy tore his pants.                                        CONFLICT

CHAPTER 3

For older children, copy the page, cut the scenes into pieces, and have small groups role-play these situations for their classmates. Ask the class to decide whether the scenes show conflict or bullying.

# 4 Creating Closure: Consequences and Apologies

You may choose to open this lesson by sharing with children the personal action plan you developed from Chapter 2. Tell children that tackling the problem of bullying is very important in your classroom and that by working together and learning new skills and strategies, your class will work toward stopping bullying behaviors and making everyone feeling safe. Review your plan, emphasizing that a plan helps you think ahead about what steps to take in a bullying situation. Let your students know they will be creating their own action plans for dealing with bullies in the next few weeks.

> Discussing consequences with children is essential; they must clearly see that the consequences you've established are predictable, immediate, and inevitable, and that the consequences will escalate if the behavior is repeated. (While consequences most often are seen as negative, there can be positive consequences for behavior as well. Read more about school-wide policies for creating consequences in Chapter 8.)

Highlight the consequences you've put into your plan. Define the word *consequences* in simple language: A consequence is something that happens because of something you've done. If you drop a glass on the floor, the consequence may be that it breaks. If you talk back to your mom, the consequence might be that you can't watch your favorite TV show. *Restitution,* or "fixing what you did," is another term that needs to be introduced. Offering real-life examples helps children understand what you mean: If you break someone's pencil, you give them a new one of yours. If you called someone a name, you apologize and ask the person to play with you at recess. Defining these words is very important; never assume children know or understand this vocabulary.

If you teach older children and are comfortable with having students give input into consequences, remind them of your classroom standards before asking them to share their ideas. You might list specific consequences on chart paper to be used as a reference during problem-solving situations; however, your students need to understand that you make the final decision. This is your job as the teacher.

Keep in mind that the most effective consequences are logical extensions of the situation. They must be reasonable, workable, and fall under your standards of behavior. If a consequence would be humiliating, embarrassing, or hurtful then it is not appropriate.

The reproducible on page 39 provides guidelines for developing consequences. Copy and add them to your resource book. This page can also be used when you meet with parents or discuss whole-school consequences

# Appropriate Consequences for Students Who Bully

**TIPS** *Consequences fall into a few basic categories: loss of privileges, time out, or modified responsibilities.*

*Children who bully must be treated with respect and never be expected to do an activity that would place them in embarrassing situations. Tailor the consequence to fit the child and the offense.*

*It's not effective to apply a consequence and then accept a shoddy or incomplete effort. Be sure that students are always supervised, no matter what the activity, and that the work performed meets an acceptable standard.*

*Whenever possible, consult parents about effective consequences for their child.*

**EXAMPLES:** *Students may*

❏ walk with a supervisor during recess/lunch and keep a tally of kind behavior they witness.

❏ miss recess to write a plan for future behavior (supervised).

❏ write a contract for future behavior, and sign it along with parents, teacher, and principal.

❏ phone their parents to explain the situation, describe the inappropriate behavior, and outline a restitution plan.

❏ (for older students) research and present a report to the class about people who believed in nonviolence—for example, Martin Luther King, Jr., Mother Teresa, or Gandhi.

❏ miss a non-curriculum activity to do a job for the teacher, school secretary, or janitor.

❏ use free time at lunch, recess, or after school to create anti-bullying posters.

❏ read an appropriate book about bullying (fiction or nonfiction), and create a book report to be presented to the principal.

❏ list the pros and cons of being a bully.

❏ make a poster showing 5 to 10 ways of being a friend to someone.

❏ create a big book for younger students in the school on the theme of how to be a friend, or how to be kind to others. Share it with those classes.

❏ maintain a "Bully Watch Zone" bulletin board, listing books, TV shows, and other media that feature bullies. Write a summary for each, showing how the problem was resolved.

for bullying with colleagues, as discussed in Chapter 8.

Whatever the consequence, bullies need to be held accountable for their actions. The task must include an explicit acknowledgment of what they did, how it affected the other person, and what they will do to change the situation. This acknowledgment and offer of restitution often take place in the context of the apology.

## MEANINGFUL APOLOGIES

In the second part of the class discussion, review what an apology is. Ask children why apologies are important. How can they tell if someone really means it?

Take the time to be explicit about how an apology should look and sound. You might act out various apologies with student volunteers. Contrast heartfelt, sincere apologies with flippant, careless ones. Be dramatic here! Have fun rolling your eyes, sighing, or falling to your knees to give a tearful apology. The more dramatic you are, the more your students will remember the lesson. I've always found that loosening up and acting a bit silly with children to drive home a point doesn't lessen their respect or affection for you—it increases it!

To integrate writing into the lesson, have second and third graders write out their apologies in the form of a friendly letter. For younger children it's enough to have them write "I'm sorry" and tell the classmate they bullied what they will do the next time instead. Older children should go into more detail. Have them include a description of what they did, an explanation of how their actions made the targeted student feel, their plan to provide restitution, and how they will treat the person in the future.

As an extended activity for older students, reread *Bailey the Big Bully* (see Part 2 of this chapter) and then have them write an imaginary apology letter from either Bailey or Kevin's point of view.

## 5 Working Together to End Bullying

Gather the class and read aloud *Nobody Knew What to Do*. Sensitively written and illustrated, this book tells the story of a boy who is being bullied and another boy who sees the bullying and reports it. Teachers, the principal, the parents, and students are all included in the solution.

Help students make a connection between the solution in this story and the personal action plan you shared. Reiterate that everyone needs to work together to end bullying.

> **Literature Link:**
> *Nobody Knew What to Do* by Becky McCain (Albert Whitman, 2001). This story links nicely to the lesson Bystanders Have the Power, Too! in Chapter 4.

To wrap up the first part of the No More Bullies! unit, lead a class activity that underscores the importance of being a team. Making a class "promise" quilt is a great way to create a lasting reminder of the goals of the lesson. You might opt to create a fabric quilt, following the step-by-step instructions below or instead try one of the alternative activities described on page 43.

## Create a Class Promise Quilt

Making a quilt is not as difficult as it sounds. If you can invite a couple of volunteers with sewing experience to help, so much the better! You might also contact a local quilters guild or club. These groups often have experts who would be pleased to visit your class and help.

### You will need:

- two flat bed sheets, one plain for the front and one patterned for the backing (Double sheets are usually the best size, but twin can work for smaller classes.)
- fabric crayons and fabric markers (permanent markers also work) **Note:** This quilt should be machine-washable; check to make sure the fabric crayons you use can be washed.

- chalk or pencil
- thread
- quilt batting
- a sewing machine
- safety pins (These prevent pokes as students handle the quilt.)

**STEP 1:** Divide the sheet into a grid. Decide how many squares you can create on the sheet, and leave at least 2 inches of material around the edges for a 1-inch border (1-inch seam allowance). The squares must be in a straight line across and down, as you will run a line of stitching down each row to finish the quilt. As you work out the placement of squares, gently marking guidelines on the quilt with chalk or pencil, leave a blank area in the middle of the sheet for the slogan and everyone's signatures.

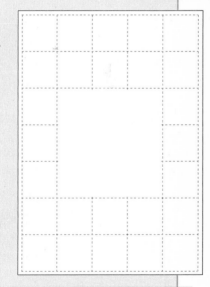

**STEP 2:** Decide on an inspiring bully-free class slogan with children, such as "We are a bully-free class." Have children use fabric crayons on computer paper cut to the correct square dimensions to draw a picture that shows their response to the slogan. You might have older children write a promise in their square and then decorate it. (Remind them that any words must be written backward so the words will face the right way when ironed!) Don't forget to create your own square, and if there are blank squares, ask your principal or other teachers who work with your class to make a contribution.

As an alternative for drawing an iron-on design in steps 2 and 4, you might have students create designs on a computer, run them off on T-shirt transfer paper, and then iron these onto the sheet.

**STEP 3:** Print the slogan or promise you've decided upon in the center of your sheet and then have each student sign his or her name around the slogan. Permanent felt pens work well for this as children don't have to write backward and the ink will stay, even if the quilt gets wet. Be sure to do the writing before you begin to sew the quilt together.

**STEP 4:** Following fabric crayon directions, iron each quilt square into place on the sheet. Use the grid you created in step 1 to guide you as you place each square.

For the next few steps, it's important to have as many students as possible help you; teamwork helps students feel proud of the finished product. Divide your class into small groups of children and before you begin to put the quilt together, plan the tasks these groups can help with. One group can help lay out batting, another can smooth wrinkles, tape the sheet to the ground, and so on. Older students can help with the pinning.

**STEP 5**

batting

**STEP 5:** Lay the batting on the floor, smoothing out any wrinkles. Lay the quilt top **right side up** on top of the batting and use safety pins to pin the whole thing to the backing all the way around (pin every square for the best result). Once pinned, trim the batting so it's the same size as the sheet.

**STEP 6**

batting side up

quilt side facing down
patterned sheet

**STEP 6:** Tape the other sheet onto the floor with masking tape, **pattern side up**. Take the batting/top quilt piece and flip it upside down onto the floor so that the two fabric pieces are touching, right sides together, and the batting is facing up so you can see it. Gently lift the tape and pin around the outside, trimming away extra batting if necessary.

**STEP 7**

batting side up

**STEP 7:** Sew around the outside (using at least a 1-inch seam allowance). Leave one end open. Remove the pins, and turn the quilt inside out through the open side so the batting is in the middle.

**STEP 8:** Pin the open edge closed, turn the raw edges under, and sew it up with the sewing machine.

**STEP 9:** Finally, run a straight line of stitching along each horizontal and vertical line of squares to create a quilt-like look. (Use contrasting thread and/or zigzag stitches to finish).

42

This activity makes a great springboard for writing. Have beginning writers draw and describe each step; have older children write a report to include in your school's newsletter. Compile the writing in a class book; attach a photo of your students with their quilt to the cover.

You'll find many wonderful uses for your class quilt—birthday children can use the quilt during reading time, children who are having a bad day can snuggle up in it. It can be draped over a couple of desks to make a quiet reading spot, or students who have successfully worked out a problem might be invited to sit on it together during an activity. Be creative. Your goal is to use the quilt every day, reminding students of the teamwork it took to create and referring to the slogan often.

● ● ●

As you conclude the lessons and activities in the first part of the No More Bullies! unit, take stock of what children have learned—how to recognize bullying and classify the types of bullying that can occur; how to distinguish between conflict and bullying; the whys and hows of consequences. Students should also be able to use appropriate vocabulary (for example, *restitution*) and demonstrate an understanding of appropriate apologies.

Most important, your students now understand that you have recognized bullying as a problem and consider it to be a serious matter; they've seen your action plan and they know that by working together they can help make your classroom a happier place to be.

Now that you've focused on bullies themselves, it's time to move on to the second part of Unit One: You Have the Power! which helps you teach children successful strategies for dealing with bullies.

**OTHER IDEAS FOR A TEAM-BUILDING CLASS PROJECT**

Have students:

- draw their quilt design on a square piece of construction paper, then tape or staple the squares together to make a paper promise quilt on a bulletin board.

- write and design their own promise on a word-processing or simple design program. Hang each "promise page" on the class bulletin board.

- make anti-bullying posters to hang in the school.

- write "ads" about bullying to be broadcast during morning announcements.

- using fabric crayons and transfer paper, draw pictures that show (or write slogans about) a bully-free classroom. These pictures can either be ironed on plain pillowcases to create stuffed pillows for the classroom, or on plain T-shirts for each child to wear.

- write raps, chants, or poems about bullying.

- bring in brown paper bags and with adult supervision, carefully turn the bag inside out, cut out a neck hole in the bottom of the bag, and a slit up the middle to create a jacket; decorate the jacket with the slogan and pictures of people treating others with kindness.

- help make a "Bully Watch Zone" bulletin board. When your class encounters examples of bullying in stories, videos, or newspapers, have them write down the title and a brief summary of the story line, including how the problem is resolved, and add it to the board.

# You Have the Power!

*Teaching Students Successful Strategies for Dealing With Bullies (The Big Four, Unit One—Part Two)*

*This chapter expands the No More Bullies! work from Chapter 3 with a focus on empowerment.*

Parent-teacher conferences had finally arrived and we all looked forward to sharing the results of many months of hard work.

I particularly looked forward to meeting with the Lewises, Ben's parents. We had met after the last bullying incident and I shared my personal action plan with them (Chapter 2). I had also mentioned that we needed to find ways to give Ben some personal strategies and that I was working on a plan to do this. We had agreed to stay in touch, but since the bullying difficulties he had been having with Chad seemed to be diminishing, we hadn't talked in a while. I was curious to see how they felt about the situation.

After discussing his academic progress, I asked them how Ben was feeling about the situation with Chad. They felt Ben seemed more settled and didn't talk as much about being bothered by Chad.

Mr. Lewis said, "There is one thing, though, that we thought we'd mention. Ben is very confident of your support now and seeing your plan impressed him. But he seems to think that the solution lies in your hands and we feel he needs to take

a little more responsibility in handling the problem himself. We're not saying we don't want you to support him but he sees you as being the solution to the bullying. While you may be his knight in shining armor now, we're trying to get him to see that he has some power in this situation, too. You aren't always going to be there!"

I had also noticed this, not just with bullying situations, but with conflict situations in general—and I'd done some thinking about it. I was comfortable stepping in and, more often than not, solving the problem—it was expedient and allowed us to get back to work quickly. However, it wasn't a long-term solution. With bullies and conflict ever-present in the world, I knew it was time to give my class some tools to deal with both.

Agreeing with the Lewises, I reminded them of our last meeting when we had realized that Ben needed some strategies to use when bullied. This situation had helped me develop the second part of my bully-proofing unit, You Have the Power! which I outlined for them and began to introduce with my class the following week.

Children like Ben need to see that they have the power to stand up to bullies. The lessons and activities that follow introduce strategies that bullied children can try when they are faced with a bully—as the target and (in the last lesson) as a bystander. The lessons are grouped as follows:

# 1 Identifying What Bullies Look For

Allow plenty of time to read aloud Judy Cox's *Mean, Mean Maureen Green*, a story that vividly illustrates the power of self-confidence. The main character, Lilley, is terrified of Maureen, an older girl on her bus. Lilley is very timid and calls herself a wimp when she fails to stand up to Maureen. A new boy, Adam, arrives and is not fazed by Maureen at all. (In fact, he plays a cruel trick on her and implicates Lilley.) Lilley sees how Adam handles Maureen but is still unable to do anything about the bullying herself. She decides to solve the problem by learning to ride her bike. As Lilley feels more confident, an unexpected encounter with Maureen helps Lilley see that she can handle the situation.

> **Literature Link:** *Mean, Mean Maureen Green* by Judy Cox. (Holiday House, 1999). Note: Because this book is 83 pages long, you may want to begin reading it the day before or break it into sections to be read throughout the day. You want to finish the story before doing the activities below.

The issue with Maureen is not clearly resolved at the end (they don't become friends) but Lilley sees things with a new perspective.

Talk about why the students feel Lilley was targeted by Maureen. You might ask guiding questions such as, *Was Lilley being bullied or was this a conflict between students? How do you know? Does anyone think that Lilley deserved to be treated like that by Maureen? Why or why not?* By now, your students should be able to recognize that Lilley was being bullied. (If there is any uncertainty during your discussion about whether this was bullying, refer to your list of types of bullying and your T-chart comparing bullying and conflict. Relate the events in the story to the charts.)

It's appropriate, at this point, to talk about why bullies may target some people and not others. However, this needs to be handled with great care—avoid details that put bullied children in the spotlight.

## WHAT BULLIES LOOK FOR

Bullies like:

- people who don't stand up for themselves.
- people who are quiet and won't tell on them.
- people who are on their own away from kids or adults.
- people who get upset easily or cry.

Bullies don't like:

- people who say "no!" in loud voices.
- people who tell and get help.
- people who play in groups and include everyone in games.

You may choose to present the information on a chart like the one at left.

On another piece of chart paper, write Lilley's and Adam's names. Ask children to suggest words that describe how each child handled Maureen. Encourage children to use colorful words to describe Adam in particular. For example, the list could include *inventive, creative, unafraid, humorous,* and *brave.* Have a poster ready with a heading such as "Powerful Words for Powerful People." Have a student transfer the words used to describe Adam onto the poster. Encourage children to name Lilley's strengths, too (for example, she is thoughtful and determined). You may need to draw these out as you go. Add these positive words to the Powerful Words list.

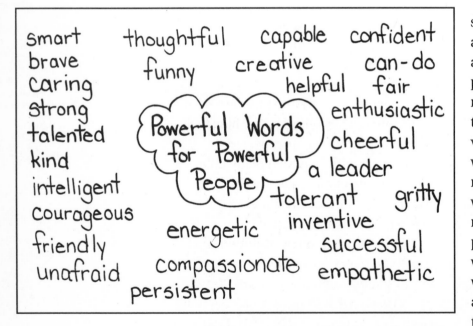

As you encounter strong, assertive story characters in other materials, add their traits to the poster. Use the poster in related language arts activities to strengthen students' vocabulary and reinforce what they've learned—you might ask older children to write poems or skipping rhymes using these powerful words or work with younger children to write a class pattern poem about a character using these words. The more you use the vocabulary, the more opportunities children have to absorb the concept of what being powerful can mean in a positive light.

To wrap up this lesson, have students draw a self-portrait, choose some powerful words from the poster to describe themselves, and then write these around the border. You might also have older students write the new "final chapter" for the book, when Lilley encounters Maureen again on the next day at school.

## 2 Creating Strategy Power Books

In lessons 3 and 4, students learn strategies to use when faced with a bullying situation. Before you begin teaching these strategies, let children create a special place to list and "own" the strategies you will discuss. I find they love to write their strategies in tiny folded paper books I call "Power Books," which are small enough to fit into a pocket. Encourage children to keep their Power Books close at hand when they're out of the classroom in case they need them.

Given a short demonstration and model, older students catch on to making Power Books quickly; I have also made these mini-books successfully with first graders. Once children "get" how to make a Power Book, they can use the format for any subject.

There are many ways to make pocket-sized books. You'll find directions for one of my favorites on page 48. Whatever format you choose, it's a good idea to have children prepare the material themselves. Making the book increases their sense of ownership and the importance they place on the information they put in the book. However, for younger children you may choose to preprint the strategies before they actually put the book together. It's also a good idea to make a couple of extra Power Books to present to those children who move into your room throughout the year. Completing a Power Book is a great activity for those students who finish assignments early.

### OTHER SIMPLE WAYS TO MAKE POWER BOOKS

- Index cards are always useful. By using the envelope setting in some computer programs, you can print information right on the card. Index cards can be three-hole-punched at the top and strung together with yarn in a figure 8 pattern. Or staple the cards together at the top and then cover with a strip of masking tape to create a top binding.

- Another type of simple booklet can be made by folding a sheet of paper in half, then in half again, then in half from top to bottom. Open the paper up and cut along each fold line, then gather the pages together and secure with a staple at the side or top of booklet.

- Long paper strips, cut from legal-size paper (or larger) can be folded accordion-style to create long booklets.

# Creating Power Books

Follow the steps below to make a Power Book. Your book will be eight pages long. If you need more than eight pages, make two books and staple one inside the other.

**1.** Use an ordinary sheet of paper. Fold it in half, top to bottom. Crease and unfold.

**2.** Fold in half, left to right. Crease it sharply, and leave it folded.

**3.** Fold again in the same direction Unfold this last step.

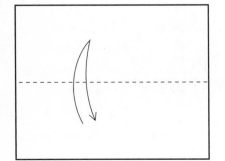

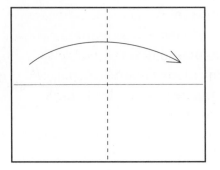

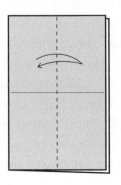

**4.** Hold the fold. Cut in from the fold to the first crease. Open the sheet.

**5.** Fold in half top to bottom, so that the two long edges meet.

**6.** Push the two outer edges in, so that the slit opens and the inner pages are formed. Crease the edges of all pages to make the book. Secure with a staple.

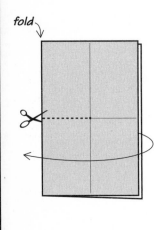

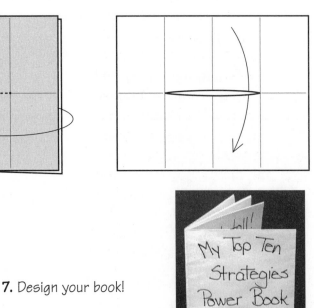

**7.** Design your book!

Activity adapted from *Origami Math* © by Karen Baicker (Scholastic, 2004) Used with permission.

Creating a Bully-Free Classroom • Scholastic Teaching Resources

# 3 Discovering What Works When a Bully Bothers You

As a first step to completing their strategy Power Books, encourage children to think about some possible ways that they can react to a bully. When you open this discussion, be sure to review your standards of behavior; as children consider appropriate responses to a bully, they need to realize that aggressive, mean-spirited replies or actions are not the best way to resolve the problem.

**Literature Link:**

*Bullies Are a Pain in the Brain* by Trevor Romain (Free Spirit Publishing, 1997)

Be aware that many storybooks and advice books about bullying offer solutions at the expense of the bully. Sarcastic comments and cruel tricks may make a funny story but the lesson they teach is a troubling one. If we expect our classrooms to be respectful, safe, and caring places for everyone, we need to make sure that this philosophy includes bullies, however hard that may be. Meeting aggression with more aggression, humiliation, or sarcasm lowers the bullied child to the same level as the bully. There are many ways to deflect a bully that don't involve nastiness, and it's important that your students realize this.

It's also very important to emphasize to children that if they ever feel as if they're in danger, they should run away and get help. In *Bullies Are a Pain in the Brain*, Trevor Romain says, "You might look a bit foolish running down the street like a maniac but you will look alive!" Children need to understand that it is never a defeat to run; in fact, in some situations it may be the smartest choice. Make sure children realize, though, that running and getting help go hand-in-hand. Emphasize that keeping quiet about a dangerous situation is *never* an option.

The following activity could be done in a few ways: You might read the Reacting to a Bully statements on page 50 and have students agree or disagree by giving a thumbs-up or thumbs-down, or giving a sideways thumb to indicate that they're not sure of the answer. You might invite a few older students into your classroom to act out these scenarios for your students, who then use their thumbs to indicate their choice. You could act out the various reactions yourself; or group children in pairs, give each pair a scenario to practice, and then let them perform for the class. Whichever format you choose, make sure you discuss each scenario in detail.

Ask students: *Is this a positive response? Why do you think it might work? Why do you think it might not work?*

Be sure to underscore the idea that there is no "magic strategy" that always works. In fact, there are many solutions children can try.

To finish this section, you may have younger students divide a page in two. On one half, ask them to draw a "thumbs-down" response to a bullying situation, and in the other, a corresponding "thumbs-up" response.

# Reacting to a Bully

*Read aloud each scenario. Have students think about the way bullying is handled and indicate that they agree (thumbs-up), disagree (thumbs-down), or aren't sure (sideways-thumb). Discuss each example. A suggested answer and explanation are given.*

**A bully calls you a name and you say in a loud voice, "Stop that. I don't deserve to be treated like that." Then you walk away.** (Thumbs-up; bullies don't like people standing up to them and using loud, assertive voices.)

**A bully is walking over to you, so you look down and hunch your shoulders so the bully won't notice you.** (Thumbs-down; a reaction like that makes a person look scared and easy to push around.)

**A bully steals your recess cookies, so you hit him and try to get them back.** (Thumbs-down; hitting him means you'll probably be the one who gets into trouble, and if the bully decides to hit you back, you may get hurt.)

**A bully has been calling you names and laughing at you, so you tell your friend.** (Thumbs-up; telling a friend is a good start because he or she can help stand up for you. It would be even better if you told your teacher or another adult, so they could help too.)

**A bully keeps tripping you when you are playing soccer. You say loudly, "Stop tripping me. I want to play soccer, not fight with you."** (Thumbs-up; bullies don't want others to know they are bullying people, and your friends on the team may stand up for you.)

**A bully makes fun of your haircut, so you make a funny joke about his/her hair.** (Sideways-thumb; sometimes a funny comment can defuse a bully's meanness but be careful not to make fun of the bully; putting down someone else or making fun of him or her makes you as bad as the bully!)

**A bully is standing behind a tree and calls for you to come over. You walk away from the bully toward a group of people on the playground.** (Thumbs-up; bullies like to use out-of-sight places to bother people. Moving closer to other people means the bullying will be seen if it continues. Besides, you don't have to do anything a bully tells you to do!)

**A bully steals your hat and you start to cry.** (Thumbs-down; some bullies like to make people cry and may see how upset they can make you.)

**A bully pulls you into an alley and threatens to beat you up unless you give him or her your jacket. You yell "Fire!" as loudly as you can and start to run as fast as you can to a place where there are other people.** (Thumbs-up; if you feel you are in a dangerous situation, running is a good choice. If you yell "Fire," people are more likely to come and see what the problem is.)

**A bully is telling your friends not to play with you at recess, so you go and join another game with other people in your class. Then you go home and tell your mom.** (Thumbs-up; walking away and joining in another game shows the bully and your friends that you won't be treated badly and that you have other friends. Telling your mom is also a great idea.)

**A bully is making your life so miserable you pretend you're sick so you can stay home from school.** (Thumbs-down; a bully would love to think he or she upset you so much you had to miss school! Plus, it means you are missing important things you should be learning. That's not fair to you.)

Creating a Bully-Free Classroom • Scholastic Teaching Resources

Invite older students to write scenarios with successful or unsuccessful strategies like those in the activity and either present them in small groups for others to vote on or prepare them as a skit with another student. You might use the students' skits as a lesson review or as an introduction to the next lesson.

# 4 The Top Ten Strategies for Handling Bullies

If you had students prepare skits or drawings in the previous lesson, you may choose to begin now by having them present their work. Follow up by telling students that they are about to learn ten great strategies for responding to bullies. They will write (or attach copies of) these strategies in their Power Book (see pages 47–48) to create a mini-reference book they can carry anywhere in their pockets.

You may introduce the following ten strategies in any order. For each one, allow children time to write the strategy in their Power Books, and model the strategy (for strategies #1 and #2, have children practice responding to you). Then have them practice with a partner, role-playing a few situations. You might want to present the ten strategies over the course of two weeks, so that children learn one each day.

> If you choose to reinforce a strategy by having students role-play, set very clear guidelines about what can be said during the role-play. Before they begin, remind children to be conscious of treating people with respect; this activity should be fun, and very cruel personal statements or comments, even in the context of the role-playing, are not acceptable. Have students keep the comments general.

## STRATEGY #1: "So?"

Begin by reading aloud, *The Meanest Thing to Say*. This story shows students that very simple responses can make very powerful strategies. Little Bill meets a new boy named Michael who challenges him to play a game called the "Twelve Meanest Things to Say to Somebody." This makes Little Bill uncomfortable and he doesn't know what to do. He tells his dad, who gives him a simple, one-word strategy: "So?" and it works. Every time Michael says something mean to Little Bill, he replies, "So?" and Michael soon becomes tired of the game.

| Literature Link: |
| --- |
| *The Meanest Thing to Say* by Bill Cosby (Scholastic, 1997) |

Let children enjoy the story a second time and practice the strategy; as you reread the book, have the class say "So?" whenever Michael says a mean thing. You might also pretend that *you* are Michael, give the students some "mean" statements ("You are all wearing ugly shoes today!"), and have them respond.

Talk about why this response is effective. (It gets boring for a bully to keep taunting if he or she simply gets the same response each time.) Remind children that it's not necessary to respond with any other word—

"So?" does the job.

Have children write this strategy in their Power Book (or if you've pre-printed these strategies in the Power Book, have them highlight it with a felt pen).

After "So?" has been added to the book, make sure your students realize that this is only one strategy. No single strategy will always work and they need to be prepared to try different responses.

### STRATEGY #2: Be a Broken Record

This is closely related to "So?" except that you choose a statement to calmly repeat over and over, such as "Stop it. I don't deserve to be treated like that." Encourage children to select a response from the "thumbs up" list you brainstormed in lesson 3. You might demonstrate how a bullying scenario would sound with the class repeating the broken-record response:

Bully: *Oh, look at your hair. Did someone cut it with a lawnmower?*

You: *Stop talking to me like that.*

Bully: *Oh, I'm scared. What are you gonna do?*

You: *Stop talking to me like that.*

Bully: *What's wrong with you? Cat got your tongue?*

You: *Stop talking to me like that.*

Bully: *"Stop talking to me like that."* (mimicking)

You: *Stop talking to me like that.*

(Bully snorts and walks off.)

### STRATEGY #3: Stand Tall!

Point out to children that how they use their bodies and voices makes a difference in how others treat them. For example, if they are hunched over, walk around looking at the ground, and use a small, whispery voice, or say "Oh, please don't do that to me. C'mon, please stop it, I don't like that. You're hurting me!" a bully may not take them seriously. Assure them that this is no time to worry about being polite.

Have children practice looking right at a partner, using a loud voice, and saying in clear terms what he or she wants the bully to do. Instead of saying "Oh, please don't do that to me!" have them practice saying loudly "Stop it. I don't like that." Together, brainstorm a list of short, direct statements children can make. If there's room, have them write a few favorites in their Power Book.

**STRATEGY #4: Breathe Deeply!**

When we are feeling scared, nervous or angry, our body's first response is to tense up. Have children show you how they look when they're scared, then angry. Point out how our bodies look when we are feeling this way (muscles clench, fists ball up, and faces grimace). When our bodies are tense, it makes it harder for our brains to think clearly. In stressful situations, learning some basic relaxation skills can help us stay calm and make good decisions about what to do. Demonstrate each step described at right.

Let children know that with practice this becomes an easy, automatic thing to do. Remind them that they may not feel they have time to do all those steps and that's okay; even just breathing deeply will help them stay calm and decide the best thing to do.

I also make sure I have children do these steps before a big exam, a concert performance, or at times when everyone is wound up and things are getting out of hand. It works!

> **Four Steps to Calm Yourself Down:**
>
> 1. Breathe deeply. Take a deep breath through your nose and hold it for a count of 4, then blow it quietly out through your mouth. As you blow out, imagine that all of your worries are blowing away through your mouth. Do this two or three times. As an alternative, you can slowly count to ten in your mind (or out loud).
> 2. Think about what you are feeling. Think about what strategy you might try first.
> 3. Breathe deeply again.
> 4. Take action.

**STRATEGY #5: Ha, Ha, Ha! (Use Humor)**

This is a sophisticated strategy and takes some practice. The aim of using humor is *not* to laugh at the bully, but to make a funny comment or joke that diffuses the situation.

Sometimes, if children are comfortable using humor, making a gentle joke about themselves can work. Give students a few positive and negative examples, such as the following: A bully is taunting you about your new haircut. It *wouldn't* be a good idea to reply, "Oh, yeah? Where'd you get *your* haircut, at Lawnmowers 'R' Us?" Instead, you could say, "Yeah, it is pretty unique and special, just like me!" or "Yeah, it kind of makes me look like Einstein, don't you think?" or "It does kind of look like I put my finger in a light socket, doesn't it?"

For younger children especially, you may need to do some group work and brainstorm funny replies. Talk with children about tone (what makes things funny but not insulting), so they can monitor their responses. This whole topic could branch out into other language arts activities such as writing joke books, creating puns, and other word-play activities.

**STRATEGY #6: Use the Eyes in the Back of Your Head!**

Developing an awareness of what is going on around them is another important strategy for children to learn. It's a wise practice in most situations for children to be watching, listening, and thinking about what is

CHAPTER 4

happening. If they see a bully (or any other potential danger) approaching, they should avoid the situation by moving to an area where there are other students or an adult. When children are aware that being off by themselves may put them in a vulnerable situation, they may make a choice to stay closer to others and circumvent problems.

If you have recess supervision, help your students practice this strategy by playing a version of "Stop, Look, and Listen!" When you blow your whistle with a special pattern only your class will recognize (practice this signal before going out) they should freeze and look around them. Are they close to others? Are they in a danger zone? Is there a classmate or group game close by that they could join? Once or twice a recess is enough to reinforce the strategy.

## STRATEGY #7: Slip Slidin' Away

One simple option children can try is walking away from a bullying situation. Encourage them not to get "hooked" into talking to the bully, but to simply turn and walk away. Tell children: If the bully steps in front of you, pivot and walk quickly away in another direction. If the bully follows, continue to pivot and turn unexpectedly until either the bully gives up or you get to a safer area. This strategy works best if you are dealing with just one person; it also works well with either "So?" or the broken record strategy.

This one is fun to practice during physical education classes, with partners taking turns playing the bully who blocks the way and the person who walks away.

## STRATEGY #8: Be Your Own Cheerleader!

Bullies like to make people feel bad about themselves; we listen to what bullies say and often believe their bad words. We all do it. How many negative comments do you remember from students and parents compared with all of the positive comments you've received during your career?

> **Literature Link:**
> *The Little Engine That Could* by Watty Piper (Grosset and Dunlap, 1978)

Positive self-talk is very effective and an empowering strategy for children to use (and comes in handy in more than just bullying situations). While it may seem a little artificial, having children repeat their strengths over and over really can contribute toward strengthening their self-confidence. In fact, reading and discussing the theme of *The Little Engine That Could*—"I think I can, I think I can . . ."—is a great way to introduce this strategy. For other activities that help children build confidence and appreciate their strengths and uniqueness, see Chapter 4, Marvelous Me!

Demonstrate how to be your own cheerleader; have a child tell you your shoes are ugly and then say to yourself (aloud so children can hear):

> "*Wow, is that bully wrong. I don't deserve to be talked to that way. I am a great person, I am kind, I would never treat anyone else that way—I don't need to because I like who I am. I like these shoes. That bully is just plain wrong!*"

Encourage children to write their own personal cheer, for example, "I am kind, I am strong, I am a good person—*I like me!*"

Give them many opportunities to practice their cheer. For example, you might add one cheer a week to the class newsletter or have them say the cheer before taking a turn in games like Red Rover.

## STRATEGY #9: Get Help

This is a strategy that should go hand-in-hand with every other strategy you teach. Training children to seek safety and guidance from someone who can help is essential.

This is a good time to clearly define the difference between telling and tattling. In *The Bully, the Bullied, and the Bystander,* Barbara Coloroso defines the difference aptly:

**Tattling:** If it will only get another person *into* trouble, don't tell me.

**Telling:** If it will get you or another child *out* of trouble, tell me.

If it is *both* (tattling and telling), I need to know. (p.135).

Use this response daily; younger children often "tell" on others, and your response should help them identify whether they are telling or tattling. You can cue them by responding, "Is this tattling or telling? Are you telling me this only to get someone else into trouble, or to get you or someone else out of trouble?"

Once children clearly understand when it's appropriate to get help, ask them to help you create a list of trustworthy people whom they can go to. At the top of the list, write your name and "your parents/caretakers." Add to the list names of other teachers, school support staff, and other adults in the school. As children write their own lists, encourage them to add trustworthy people in their community (for example, their minister).

Make sure that children think about who would be able to help; an older brother's best friend is probably not a good choice. As well, you should let people in your school know that they are on your list and to be ready if approached by a student. Hopefully, your entire school will be working together on bully-proofing but if you're not sure, talk to these people before you add them to the list.

Hang the list in a prominent place in your classroom.

## STRATEGY #10: Befriend the Bully

This strategy may seem strange but at times being friendly to a bully can make a difference.

Read the book *Bully* to your class. Mickey is harassed by Jack, a boy who steals his cookies, breaks his pencil, and is generally mean, especially

**CHAPTER 4**

since Jack's new baby brother arrived. Mickey's dad listens and gives him ideas to stand up to Jack but Mickey is so intimidated he doesn't try them. His mother suggests "Love thine enemy" and his sister agrees, telling him

> **Literature Link:**
> *Bully* by Judith Caseley (Greenwillow Books, 2001)

to take extra cookies for Jack. This is the first step toward making Jack a friend. Mickey's best strategy turns out to be "make him laugh," which helps turn Jack into a buddy.

It's very important for students who may try this to feel that the bully may be approachable (some are not!) and children should realize that, as with everything else, there are no guarantees. However, point out that even if a full-fledged friendship doesn't develop, by extending a friendly gesture you may make it harder for a bully to target you—people generally don't attack a person who is being kind to them.

This strategy is also a great lead-in or support to the friendship component, discussed in Chapter 6.

It is always appropriate to encourage children to share other strategies that they use or may think of during these discussions. Assure them that there are more than the ten strategies they've just learned and strive to include children's practical ideas whenever you can.

Now that these strategies are in place, and in the children's Power Books, make sure that you revisit each one consistently over the upcoming months.

## 5 Creating a Personal Action Plan (Student Version)

This student-created action plan for dealing with bullies is related to the action plan you have created but is much simpler.

You may choose to show the personal bully-proofing plan that you created in Chapter 2 on the overhead projector; as you share it with your class, talk about the steps you went through to create it, and how the plan helps you feel in control because you know what you plan to do.

Next, share the outline that they will follow to create their plan. (Use the reproducible fill-in plan provided on page 57 or create your own version.) Remind children that, as with all plans, their course of action needs to be flexible; that is, a situation may arise where following their plan doesn't make sense. Generally, though, the plan gives children a way to begin to solve the problem.

For this activity, you might let children work on their plan individually or with a trusted partner. Pair younger children with a buddy from a higher grade. For example, first graders and sixth graders seem to enjoy each other's company.

# _____'s Action Plan

If I'm being bullied, first I will

_____

_____

_____

_____

And then I will tell _____

If that doesn't work, then I will try _____

_____

_____

And then I will tell _____

My emergency strategy will be

_____

_____

_____

And I will get help by telling _____

• • •

If I ever feel that I am in danger, I will run away
and tell an adult RIGHT AWAY!

To begin, distribute copies of page 57 and have children fill in the plan outline, choosing the two strategies they feel most comfortable with from their Power Book. The third or "emergency" strategy is any strategy a child is willing to try as a last resort. As they fill in the plan, younger students may draw pictures while their helper adds the words underneath. It's very important to make sure that each child does his or her own work on the plan and that the partner merely supports this work; each child needs to feel ownership for his or her plan.

After the plan is filled in, invite children to decorate it. I recommend buying big golden award seals (available in office supply stores) and ribbon to add to the bottom to make the plans appear "official."

The last step of this plan is to have children sign the bottom, date it, and then have you sign it as well. Make a big deal out of this step; you might invite the buddy class and even your principal to a signing ceremony and serve punch and cookies or popcorn. If children are excited and enthusiastic about their plan, they are likely to use it.

Make copies of these plans to send home; the originals could be hung on a bulletin board. Older students can make another Power Book (page 48) and copy their plan into it so it's close at hand.

To conclude the buddy activity, have the older student help the younger partner practice his or her plan a few times. Otherwise, build in some time for children to practice in pairs.

## 6 Building Group Skills: Bystanders Have the Power, Too!

Open this final lesson by reading aloud *The Hundred Dresses*. This thought-provoking story shows how bystanders can make a difference to children who need help. Maddie, Peggy, and their female classmates make fun of

> **Literature Link:**
> *The Hundred Dresses* by Eleanor Estes (Harcourt Brace, 1972)

Wanda, a girl who is poor and wears the same dress day after day. Maddie feels uncomfortable about teasing Wanda, who obviously wants to be part of the group, but she doesn't want to go against Peggy and her friends. Wanda insists she has 100 dresses at home and that turns out to be true but by the time the girls discover the truth, Wanda's family has moved because of the bullying. Maddie learns an important lesson about the power of bullies and bystanders.

Take this opportunity to create a class ethos that encourages children to look out for each other, include each other in activities, and be aware of what is happening to their classmates. While you will cover this material in more detail in Chapter 6, it is appropriate to introduce the concept that as bystanders children can make a difference. Students must realize that bullying will stop only when bullied children and bystanders refuse to let it continue. Bullies rely on children who see but don't intervene; bystander inaction allows and even encourages the bully to continue to harass others. When bystanders step in or involve others in positive activities, bullies don't have a chance.

Follow up *The Hundred Dresses* discussion with activities that stress looking out for classmates and caring about others—ways to convey the message that your class is a type of family. You might have children create a class pledge to include others in recess games, and create posters, buttons, or stickers with the same message.

By becoming involved in a positive way, your students can make a difference. In a class discussion, define *bystander* and explain the four types of bystander behaviors outlined in the box at right.

On a piece of chart paper or on an overhead, list the four bystander behaviors and ask children to think about the books about bullying the class has read so far. Have students recall examples of bystanders from each book, and list where the responses of characters who are bystanders would go on the chart. For example, in *Mean, Mean Maureen Green* the bus driver is a bystander. (Let children know that adults can be bystanders, too.) The bus driver sees and hears Maureen's threats on the bus, but does nothing. The driver's response probably fits best into "C." With *The Hundred Dresses*, decide where Maddie's behavior would fit.

> Bystanders are people who see the bullying happening. They usually do one of four things:
>
> A) join in the bullying.
>
> B) enjoy watching the bullying, but don't help the bully.
>
> C) don't like the bullying but don't know how to help.
>
> D) step in, stand up, and get help for the person being bullied.

With each example, have students think about how the bullying situation would have changed if a bystander had stepped in to help. Would Bailey in *Bailey the Big Bully* have been a bully if the students had stepped in and gotten help before Max had arrived? What do they think would have happened if the bus driver had given Maureen Green consequences for her bus behavior? What could have happened if other children on the playground had stepped in and told Michael not to play "The Twelve Meanest Things to Say?"

Beginning with examples from the "Conflict or Bullying?" scenarios on page 37, make a list of things students could say or do when intervening. Quite a few of the Top Ten Strategies work for bystanders, too. Add these to the list.

Remind children that body language plays a large role here, too. Standing straight, looking the bully in the eye, and using a loud, strong voice really lets everyone know you mean what you say.

Once you've used the bullying examples on the sheet and worked through a couple of solutions for bystanders, you and your class may decide to write a few more bullying situations and then have groups of

**CHAPTER 4**

four or five practice their responses with one student playing the bully, one playing the bullied child, and two or three playing the bystanders. (Younger students may create paper-bag puppets to use when practicing their responses in a group.) Encourage groups to try a variety of solutions listed on the chart paper or add new ideas. Stress the need for students to be flexible; there is never just one way to solve a problem.

To wrap up this lesson, you may want to have students add a new section to their Power Book to list their best bystander intervention strategies or you might have them highlight those strategies already listed in their Power Book that they think are good ones to use when intervening in a bullying situation.

> As always, it's important for students to remember that all examples and solutions must fit into your standards of behavior, and everyone must always be treated with respect, even when role-playing.

Depending on your class, you may also choose to have children create a personal bystander action plan, modeled on the bullying plan. Have children fill in the same template, according to the strategies they've practiced.

By now, you've introduced children to a lot of useful information about bullying. They understand the characteristics of bullies and have a plan and a list of strategies to try if a bully targets them. If they see someone else being bullied, they understand the importance of stepping in and have practiced how to respond.

Your students should be realizing that in your classroom, each person's behavior affects others and that by being a "family" and caring about others, they can help reduce or stop bullying of class members.

As well, children should be feeling more confident about their abilities when dealing with a bullying situation. The lessons and strategies in the next chapter, Marvelous Me! are designed to further nurture students' self-confidence as they celebrate the things that make them special and discover their unique strengths.

# Marvelous Me!

## *(The Big Four: Unit Two)*

The results of our bully-proofing activities were beginning to show. Children were reporting fewer problems on the playground and I had observed my students reading and rereading their Power Books during both free time and recess. I saw a few of the children continuing to role-play bullying episodes and practice their strategies while playing on the playground. Students from other classes were noticing and asking questions.

Chad's bullying behavior continued to be an issue for others but seemed to be decreasing. Ben seemed more comfortable with Chad but was tentative and unsure of himself when handling conflicts in our classroom.

In fact, I was becoming concerned about Ben's view of himself. He would often refer to himself as a "dummy," mutter that he wouldn't be able to do a new activity, or give up on unfamiliar or challenging work when he was overwhelmed. While I saw Ben as a competent learner, he obviously didn't.

Socially, Ben didn't have a "best" friend in our room and preferred to hang around on the fringes of an activity. This lack of confidence and uncertainty about friendships was also having an effect on Ben's view of himself as a likeable, competent person.

I saw Ben's mom in the hall one afternoon, and mentioned my observations to her. She had noticed these things, too, and was frustrated by his poor self-image.

"Even though we see Ben as doing well academically, I don't think he feels successful," I suggested. "What is he really good at? It doesn't have to be academic; anything that Ben loves and feels good about can help increase his

confidence in general." I explained that when kids feel successful, it gives them the feeling that they are capable people. When they feel they are competent, they can handle new things; it gets easier to face new challenges—and bullies.

She agreed that Ben tended to be a bit of a loner so they hadn't tried to get him involved in many other activities. He always talked about his uncle's swimming pool; could he join a swim club? We brainstormed for a few minutes, and Mrs. Lewis agreed to help Ben find some new group experiences that would give him opportunities to meet new people.

As well, I suggested that the Lewises give Ben some consistent responsibilities around the house. I explained that having responsibilities would increase Ben's sense of competence. The chores would have to be important tasks, and Ben needed to know that his family would rely on him to do these jobs.

While it seemed a little out of my realm to be giving advice about chores, I felt strongly that this would have an impact on Ben's overall view of himself. If he saw himself as being a competent, responsible person, he might feel and act less vulnerable in general—and in bullying situations, specifically.

Because the benefits of celebrating students' strengths are clear, this seemed to be a perfect opportunity to provide many opportunities for Ben and his classmates to feel valued, cared for, and capable. As Barbara Coloroso says in *The Bully, the Bullied, and the Bystander*, "Children are buffered from the possible impact of a bully, or from the need to become a bully, by the daily reinforcement of the messages that foster a

*Helping students learn to respect their own strengths and uniqueness and the uniqueness of others is the goal of this chapter.*

**CHAPTER 5**

strong sense of self: I like myself. . . . I can think for myself."

The unit I embarked on next places an emphasis on self-confidence and feelings of self-worth. It connects to and builds on the personal bully-proofing strategies discussed in Chapter 3, particularly "Be Your Own Cheerleader."

Helping students learn to respect their own strengths and uniqueness, and the uniqueness of others, is the goal of this chapter. Through experiences with literature, strategy lessons, and discussion-based activities, you'll find ways to help children develop an awareness of how people experience emotions differently and feel connected to others. The activities in this unit help foster children's sense of respect and empathy, and cultivate the feeling that they belong to a "family" in your classroom. Children also gain satisfaction from learning to take responsibility and feel successful when they meet the expectations and needs of others. This theme should provide opportunities for bullied children in particular to feel capable, confident, and valued.

This chapter helps you plan a Marvelous Me! unit in six parts:

1: Using Commercial Materials

2: Introducing Vocabulary That Describes Emotion

3: Recognizing and Celebrating Individuality

4: Developing Positive Relationships With Authority Figures

5: Developing Personal Responsibility in the Classroom

6: Supporting Children Who Need Positive Experiences

> **All About Me** is a theme that many teachers use to start the year, and with good reason. Having children share their interests and talents is a wonderful way to begin learning what makes each child tick. However, as with all of the units in this book, you may begin at any time of the year. Remember that these strategies should be reinforced and built upon throughout the year to ensure that children always feel successful and appreciative of their own uniqueness.

# 1 Using Commercial Materials

The activities in this chapter can be used to supplement the character-education resources or materials you may already use. There are many published themes or unit packages available that provide a broader framework for Marvelous Me!—a variation on the All About Me theme—and any good package will allow students to think about themselves in new ways. The interactive lessons that follow provide students additional opportunities to focus on what they do well and what they are proud of—as well as recognize the ways each classmate is unique.

Creating a Bully-Free Classroom • Scholastic Teaching Resources

Here are three key tips to keep in mind when integrating commercial programs into your bully-proofing work:

**Beware of activities that don't allow children to honestly share information.** Fill-in-the-blank worksheets and other scripted activities restrict what children can communicate. The exception to this may be for kindergarten and beginning first graders or ESL students who need a framework to share their ideas. Ensure that if they use patterned or prepared work sheets, your students have an opportunity to expand their ideas using pictures and discussion.

**Consider what parts of the unit relate to your students' experiences. Be sure when discussing students' families to offer open-ended responses and accept all types of families.** Materials with strong biases toward traditional families may place students from non-traditional families in an awkward position. Choose materials wisely so that every activity is a positive experience for all of your students.

**Make sure that you celebrate and focus on children's achievements in *all* areas of their lives.** Too often, we tend to focus on academic achievement or success in sports. However, children need to see that it's terrific to be able to hop one hundred times on one foot, just as it's terrific to be good at your times tables. In fact, I advise searching for and celebrating those student strengths that are not necessarily school-related. For children who do not find it easy to excel in academic subjects, realizing that they have other strengths and accomplishments in other areas can make a huge difference in the way they view themselves.

Before you begin the lessons that follow, review your standards of behavior with children (see Chapter 2). As children share personal, important things in their lives, make sure that their peers show respect; it is effective to spend a full class discussion on this issue and establishing consequences for children who laugh at or put down others during these

**CHAPTER 5**

happy
glad    jolly
blissful    merry
cheerful
light-hearted
joyful
pleased
gleeful
genial
delighted
"tickled pink"
exhilarated

mad
angry    sore
furious
outraged
offended
exasperated
upset
ticked-off
"hot under the
collar"
"mad as a
hornet"

activities. You may choose to ask for student input or simply review consequences for this behavior. As with all parts of your plan, it pays to take time to establish your expectations for behavior.

It's also very important for you to share things about yourself. If we expect our students to tell us about their feelings and successes, we also need to take part. Besides, children are thrilled to learn more about you, their teacher, and this contributes to the feeling of togetherness that you are working to achieve.

The following activities are meant to put the spotlight on each child's strengths and interests and to enhance the activities suggested in readily-available materials. The goal is for students to realize that while we are all the same in some ways, each of us is unique, special, and different in our own way. Celebrate these differences!

## 2 Introducing Vocabulary That Describes Emotion

Read aloud *What Makes Me Happy?* This simple book offers an easy way to open a discussion about emotions and introduce related vocabulary concepts that are particularly important for younger and ESL children.

> **Literature Link:**
> *What Makes Me Happy?* by Catherine and Laurence Anholt (Candlewick Press, 1995)

Each page focuses on a different emotion: What makes me happy? What makes me sad? What makes me angry? What makes me laugh? The authors ask questions and then give examples of things that can make a person experience each emotion. Use *What Makes Me Happy?* as a springboard to introduce the idea that while we all experience the same emotions, each of us responds differently to our world—different things make us happy, sad, or angry.

As you read and discuss the book, compile a list of vocabulary words that describe feelings. Too often, we allow students to use generic words like *happy, sad,* or *mad.* The lists you create can encourage children to use a wide range of descriptive words both to help children develop a rich vocabulary and to nurture their ability to express themselves accurately and appropriately.

I make giant pencil shapes, one for each basic emotion. On the "happy" pencil, we list as many synonyms as possible for happiness. I call these "zippy word" pencils and encourage students to select words from these lists to use in their writing and their conversation. If you have a computer center, you might introduce children to the thesaurus in the word processing program. Older children can be introduced to that old-fashioned resource, the thesaurus in book form.

Any time you encounter words that describe emotions in books or passages you are reading with the class, add them to the zippy word lists. The lists you create will come in handy for children both during language arts instruction and during your conflict resolution unit (Chapter 7), so post them prominently in your room.

If children need additional practice naming emotions, have them create their own reference booklet about emotions (see book-making ideas on page 34). Using *What Makes Me Happy?* as a model, children can begin each page with the question "What Makes Me _____?" and write and illustrate their answers. (Encourage older students to use zippy words from the pencils to create their emotion books.) You might give younger children sentence frames in a booklet to complete, using basic emotions vocabulary. Or you might have them use a frame like the following to write a "feelings" poem about themselves:

_____makes me happy,

_____makes me sad,

_____makes me silly,

and _____makes me mad!

## 3 Recognizing and Celebrating Individuality

Included in this section are four activities that help children find and share their unique likes and dislikes, talents, and skills with others. The special things they share become a sort of currency for building friendships and provide social status in the classroom.

### BORING!

In a class discussion, help children understand that their feelings are unique to them, and that not feeling what everyone else feels is okay. (If students completed "feelings" booklet entries or poetry from the last lesson, invite them to share their writing with a partner. Partners can discuss whether they feel similarly or differently about the same things.)

Introduce the word *unique* and discuss the many ways someone could be unique. Talking about favorite things is a good place to help children understand what you mean. Tell children (with a little embellishment) what unusual favorite food or song makes you ecstatic. (Use those zippy words!)

Talk about the opposite of being unique. Have students consider the following questions: What would it be like to have a world where everyone looked the same? Acted the same way? Liked the same things? Read the same books? What could happen if everyone had exactly the same running shoes? Ate the same food for lunch every day?

Brainstorm ideas for a "same" day with children. They may come up with ideas such as everyone wearing the same colors, eating the same

Food is a topic of conversation for uncovering unique likes and dislikes. For example, most children will say that they love pizza, brownies, or "passgetti." I let children know that warm chicken liver salad makes me happy. You can imagine the response I get, but I make sure that I explain why. In my best Julia Child impression, I describe the tangy dressing, the crunchiness of the lettuce and the warm, melting softness of the sautéed livers. I want them to realize that I'm really serious and I think it's kind of neat that I like something that other people may not appreciate. Liking that warm chicken liver salad certainly makes me unique!

recess snack (provided by you), or trying to draw a picture exactly the same as your example. If you can organize and coordinate such a day, children will find that after a while, sameness can be frustrating and dull.

You might work with the physical education teacher to plan a "same and different" class where students work with the idea of "marching to the beat of a different drummer." Movement activities might include having children first march around at exactly the same time and in the same way. Then when they've discovered how tiring this can be, have each child invent his or her own marching pattern or way of walking. With older students, this may be an appropriate time to talk about peer pressure and how the way you feel about yourself can impact the amount of influence your friends have on you, or vice versa.

When you conclude this activity, remind children that sometimes it *is* better to be "in step" with others. You might even teach a simple group activity such as a 4-step line dance or a simple square dance pattern to drive home this point. What would happen if everyone did his or her own thing in a line dance situation, in the school choir, or in a game like soccer or baseball? On a piece of chart paper, brainstorm times when it's better to do something the same way as others and times when it's best to be unique.

### WOW! I'M FABULOUS

This is a terrific language arts–based activity that not only celebrates each child's uniqueness, but introduces some wonderful vocabulary and descriptive phrasing as well.

### Here are some other ideas you may want to try with your class:

- Create a class slogan: "Being the Same Is Boring!" or "I'm Not Boring, I'm Me!" There are many ways of sharing this slogan with others, including having students write the slogan on t-shirts and draw pictures that show their unique qualities (as with the quilt in Chapter 3, have them write with permanent markers directly on the fabric or create a design with fabric crayons on computer paper for an iron-on transfer).

- Make a mural for the hallways with your slogan and pictures of ways people in your class are unique.
- Write a rap or skipping chant to share at an assembly.
- Create a banner for your classroom out of an old sheet or plain fabric; students can decorate it using felt pens.

> **Literature Links:**
>
> *Incredible Me!* by Kathy Appelt (Harper Collins, 2003)
>
> *ABC, I Like Me!* by Nancy Carlson (Viking, 1997)

Read aloud *Incredible Me!*, a poem that describes all of the special and unique things that the narrator thinks about herself. While some phrases or words may need to be explained to young children or ESL students, the exuberance of the language makes this a fun read.

**Nobody's cowlick stands up like mine,**
**Nobody's freckles are this divine**
**I'm the cream in the butter,**
**I'm the salt in the sea,**
**I'm the one, the only, spectacular ME!**

(from Incredible Me! © 2003 by Kathy Appelt)

Create a class "Incredible Us" poem using this pattern, focusing on the special attributes your class shares, such as

Nobody's science experiments surprise us quite like ours,
Nobody's chants are as loud and superb . . . !

(Remind children to refer to the zippy words lists as they write.) This is an excellent opportunity to turn your class poem into a choral piece for an assembly. It could also be written in a big book format and used for language arts lessons or independent reading.

In addition to or as an alternative to *Incredible Me!*, read aloud *ABC, I Like Me!* A different kind of alphabet book, it has a narrator who celebrates her unique personality with each letter of the alphabet, beginning with "I am **A**wesome, **B**rave and **C**heerful." Have children use this book as a model and create their own *ABC, All About Me!* book.

## YAHOO, LOOK WHAT I CAN DO!

This activity grew out of one of my least favorite weekly activities, which was, coincidentally, one of the most beloved by my students: Show and Tell. I saw Show and Tell as a showcase for some of my luckier students to share their latest acquisitions while my less fortunate children gazed in envy. Yahoo, Look What I Can Do! provided a wonderful solution: all children were able to participate in a less "commercial" event that still provided the necessary opportunity for children to be proud of something in their lives and practice speaking and listening skills.

To kick off this alternative activity, encourage each member of the class to think about a talent, skill, or piece of knowledge he or she might share. You might begin by brainstorming a list of things that would be interesting

*Not every child will feel comfortable at first getting up in front of the class, and they must never be forced to take part. I find, though, that when they see the interest and supportive response of the class, eventually everyone in the room will participate.*

**CHAPTER 5**

for children to learn about one another. The emphasis must be on a wide variety of activities, and it's important to stress that everyone is good at something.

Once your idea list is finished, post it in a conspicuous place in your room and then put a sign-up sheet in a prominent place. To build enthusiasm, send home a reminder in your daily or weekly newsletters and schedule your own sharing time. In my classroom, throughout the week I often mention something on the idea list and wonder out loud whether someone will be doing this at "Yahoo!" time this week. And when I decide to participate, I always make a big deal out of adding my name to the list.

To really get this going, I recommend doing two things:

- Take part. Share something yourself every time for the first month or so and then regularly throughout the rest of the year.
- If at all possible, either videotape each session (very handy to show to parents during parent-teacher conferences as they wait to meet with you) or photograph every student in action and then post the pictures on a bulletin board display, called the "Yahoo!  Look What I Can Do" board.

This activity is guaranteed to be a winner. In our classroom, my students love the chance to shine and share something special they can do or teach us something we don't know. Often, students become class "experts" who are called upon for help or advice. One year, a boy (who was quiet and timid) brought in his rock collection and shared his knowledge of geology, and particularly his special rock that had "Fool's Gold" embedded inside. For months afterward, children brought him rocks from the playground and he always carefully looked at their findings to see whether or not they had found some gold of their own.

## KING OR QUEEN OF THE DAY

This activity works very well for younger children, but can be easily adapted for older children. Every day, one child is chosen to be "king" or "queen" of the day; the outgoing monarch draws the new name. I recommend conducting this activity on consecutive days for a month or until each child has had a turn; waiting for

## Your list might include:

- Playing the piano
- Doing a simple acrobatic or endurance activity (hopping on one foot 50 times)
- Dancing
- Singing
- Sharing your rock collection and teaching us about rocks
- Blowing a huge bubble with bubble formula
- Sharing a science experiment
- Performing card or magic tricks
- Sharing a picture you drew
- Sharing a piece of work you are very proud of
- Reading a story you have written
- Showing karate moves learned at karate lessons
- Sharing cookies that you baked
- Showing pictures of your pet and talking about what you do to take care of it

A few days prior to each session, consult with children who have signed up to see whether they need a special space or equipment. With advance planning you can often accommodate their needs, such as setting up an area for an experiment or borrowing a keyboard.

each child's birthday takes all year and diffuses the excitement and social learning that takes place in a concentrated period of time.

In the morning your focus on the king or queen can easily be tied into language arts. For the remainder of the morning (or afternoon) allow the monarch to call on peers to answer questions, hand out assignments, head the line for the hallway, or have another privilege you feel is appropriate.

For beginning first graders, we examine the new monarch's name and tie in the concepts we've discussed so far. We look for little words "hiding" inside, chant the spelling, search for short vowels—you name it, we see and discuss it. Then, we look at the names of the previous monarchs, listed in alphabetical order, and decide where the new name fits.

Next, we write about the king or queen. On the computer (using the largest font so everyone can see what's being written) or chart paper, we record the monarch's answers to a series of questions about him- or herself. These questions are always the same, eliciting name and age, family information (number of family members, siblings, pets), favorites (food, TV show, color, book), talents, and finally, one important thing that the class should know about the king or queen. The king or queen dictates the answers to be typed. Use this opportunity to model writing and editing skills.

If you are using the computer, make each answer a new page to create a simple book for the child. For example,

*"Queen" Zoe sits in the "throne" (my chair), wearing a crown and a cape used by each "monarch." Magic wands or scepters are optional.*

**ALL ABOUT KING BILLY**
- King Billy is six years old.
- He has five people in his family. King Billy has two big sisters. He has a cat named Maurice.
- King Billy loves to eat pizza. He doesn't watch TV.
- King Billy is very good at soccer.
- King Billy loves to be in first grade. Someday he wants to be a soccer coach.

**CHAPTER 5**

Make three copies of the book; one for the child, one for the class-room library, and one for the child to give to someone special. During the afternoon, or at a quiet time, have the monarch choose two children to help illustrate the books. You also might wait until everyone has been chosen and then have children spend an afternoon illustrating the copies, rereading the books, and sharing them with others.

Be sure to create a special spot for these books to be kept. You want to encourage your students to read these books during independent reading or for a free time activity. They will be very popular!

## 4 Developing Positive Relationships With Authority Figures

Too often, children encounter the principal or administrators in your school rarely and usually not for pleasant reasons. It makes a huge differ-ence, for both students and administrators, to have a good relationship with each other. Several informal interactions allow principals to establish a much-needed positive connection with children who may bully others or have behavior difficulties. As well, bullied children who have met infor-mally with the principal have a chance to see administrators as non-threatening people they can ask for help. Finally, regular student-administrator meetings set a positive tone in the school. (What a great experience to have your principal know your name and be interested in you as a person!)

Here is a simple way to develop this relationship: Ask your principal to set aside five or ten minutes at some point during his or her admittedly hectic day for students to visit. It doesn't have to be every day; sending one student one day a week works well. The purpose of these visits is to have each child share with the principal something special, such as terrific work they have done, a new skill they have learned, or something they've created like the king/queen books. If you can arrange to have a picture taken of the student with the principal, so much the better. Supply him or her with small award certificates to thank the student who visited.

To effectively manage student visits, be sure to keep a discreet list of who needs a chance to visit; jot the names of students on your lesson plan if you notice something they could share the following day. Keep track of who goes because children definitely will!

It's also very important to make sure that your students make visits for real accomplishments, not just because they haven't gone yet. Kids know when they are truly being rewarded for something they have done; make sure it's a meaningful experience.

Creating a Bully-Free Classroom • Scholastic Teaching Resources

# 5 Cultivating Personal Responsibility in the Classroom

If we ask parents to ensure that children learn to take responsibility for chores at home, then we need to make sure this is part of our classroom routine as well. Providing appropriate responsibilities in the classroom allows children to feel competent and successful—feelings that they are able to carry into other areas of their lives. A confident child is less likely to be bullied!

Children need to feel that their contribution is essential and for that reason the jobs that they do must have some sort of impact in the class. A library monitor who forgets to return the library books will quickly realize how important the job is when the list of overdue books is received. The blackboard monitor will need to be on the ball when he or she sees you standing at the board, chalk in hand, perplexed because there is no chalkboard space to write on.

Make a list of classroom jobs that you need to have done. I find it too unwieldy and difficult to have a job for every student. Five jobs are about right, and the children change every week. Let students choose the job they wish to be responsible for (unless someone is always taking a certain job and then a quiet conversation about being fair to others is in order).

Whatever jobs you offer, children must see that their contribution is important and necessary for the smooth operation of the classroom. Having a small thank-you note for each student at the end of the week is an important acknowledgement that you value his or her help.

## Possible jobs include:

- Blackboard Monitor (erases the board after lessons and at end of day)
- Paper People (hand out all paper or materials)
- Library Monitors (gather and return library books)
- Class Pet Parent (feeds, cleans, and monitors pets)
- Computer Whiz (turns computers on/off, keeps area tidy)
- Mail Carrier (hands out all papers that go home or puts them in student mailboxes)
- Special Buddy (responsible for gathering copies of all missed work, and notices, in a special folder for absent students)

# 6 Supporting Children Who Need Positive Experiences

While you have jobs for your students to do in your classroom, children who desperately need some positive attention and a healthy dose of self-esteem may benefit from having extra, special activities. Take the time to emphasize how much you need their help, and show your appreciation for a job well done. The key is to make sure they realize their contribution was meaningful to you and made a difference.

Taking messages to other teachers, setting up paint or art materials, watering your favorite plant, or being the "official" pencil sharpener for

**CHAPTER 5**

your class allows students to be responsible in a special way, particularly if they are children who don't get enough positive reinforcement at school.

A useful job for children who wiggle or can't control their behavior while in a group situation is holding your instructional tools—chalk, felt pens, or book—until you need them. This responsibility has really made a difference to some of my students who've needed support with self-control; being my assistant helped them focus on the lesson—and doing their job well.

Some children really blossom when they are asked to help younger students in some way. You might arrange for a student to work with a younger child daily for a short period of time on a specific need. For example, over the course of two weeks, he or she could work on addition basic facts with a "study buddy" for ten minutes a day.

I have seen many students who had difficulty controlling their behavior in my classroom settle down and become a responsible, enthusiastic "teacher" of a younger child. One boy I taught caused upheaval in my classroom whenever he could. With reluctance but cautious optimism, I asked him to be a "study buddy" to a kindergarten child who needed help learning his colors. This boy became so enthusiastic, he invented color lessons at home and his excitement when his buddy learned his colors was something to see. He helped a few other students and always deserved the glowing comments and praise from the students and teachers involved. While he still faced behavior challenges in our classroom, he felt successful and became more cooperative and pleasant to be around.

● ● ●

Every time a student feels good about his or her efforts, you can be sure it's another step toward building a positive view of him- or herself. Children who bully gain from these experiences as well. Bullies need to feel powerful. Knowing they are liked and respected by others because of the positive things they do can have a huge impact on their behavior and view of others. Children feel powerful when they assume responsibility for their decisions and meet the expectations of others—and are proud of themselves for these accomplishments.

All of these activities will go a long way toward helping your students feel successful and positive about themselves and their accomplishments. Never pass up an opportunity to shine a positive spotlight on someone, and never miss a chance to tell your students what wonderful, unique and talented people they truly are.

Now that your students are "tuned in" to each other, and are beginning to appreciate one another's talents and interests, it is appropriate to focus on interpersonal relationships. Learning about how to make and keep friends becomes the focus in the next unit, Fabulous Friends.

# Fabulous Friends

## *(The Big Four, Unit Three)*

As the class practiced bully-proofing strategies and gained confidence through the Marvelous Me! activities we'd begun, I began to think about how our bully-proofing and self-esteem-building activities had affected Claire and Sean, my other "problem" students.

Claire from California still attempted to be the queen bee of her group. Though some of the girls she had bullied no longer hung around with her and her sphere of influence had diminished, the girls who remained in the group seemed reluctant to disagree with Claire and succumbed to her use of exclusion and threats to keep them in line. They were paying a high price for this "friendship." I made plans to review types of bullying and emphasize Marvelous Me! work to help each girl see herself as a likeable person who deserved to be treated well. In tandem, I wanted to find ways to encourage them to initiate friendships with others in the classroom—and build healthier, happier relationships.

Sean, my AD/HD student, was still having a lot of difficulty dealing with others in a positive way; it appeared that most of my children were trying the "Use the eyes in the back of your head" strategy and avoiding him altogether. This solved their problem, but didn't do much for Sean.

Sean had been on Ritalin for a few weeks, and the difference was apparent. He was able to focus for longer periods of time and his work was beginning to show improvement. Now it would be easier for him to focus on learning and practicing how to make and keep friends, and he needed lots of help with social skills. We were lucky enough to have a resource teacher who agreed to work with Sean and a few others on developing skills that would enable them to deal successfully with their peers. It would be a long process but at least Sean was ready to begin.

The common thread between these situations was my students' lack of knowledge about friendship: how to make and keep friends.

In fact, children often need explicit instruction about developing and maintaining friendships. Both bullies and bullied children in particular benefit from learning how to be a friend. Activities that promote aspects of healthy friendships, such as developing mutual interests and caring for each other, give students the ability to understand how wonderful good friends can be. The girls in Claire's group, for example, needed to understand the benefits of a supportive relationship instead of settling for a one that was unequal, unstable, and negative. This became the basis for the third unit of my bully-proofing plan.

*As in the Marvelous Me! unit, there are many valuable resources available on the topic of friendship. The following lessons and activities can supplement materials you may already have and provide further opportunities for allowing children to explore and practice relationship skills. This unit is organized in five lessons.*

Initiating and maintaining successful relationships are important skills that children can learn, practice, and improve on. Knowing how to make a friend, recognizing qualities of a good friendship, and handling problems that occur between friends are important social skills that help students accept, empathize with, and respect others.

Children who exhibit these skills have a great advantage; being comfortable making and keeping friends has a huge impact on a child's self-image as a capable, likeable person. Lonnie Michelle, a leading authority on child behavior, writes:

"Kids who are skilled at making friends have many advantages over most children. The ability to make friends helps a child build a healthy self-esteem at a very early age. Children who make friends easily tend to be happier and feel better about themselves. If your child is fortunate enough to learn these skills when they are young, there is a strong likelihood that he or she will . . . have healthy self-esteem throughout life." In particular, children who bully seem to lack an understanding of how friendship works, and the main goal of any theme about getting along with other people must be to develop tolerance, respect, and empathy for others. As well, all children need opportunities to discuss, observe, and practice these skills.

As in the Marvelous Me! unit, there are many valuable resources available on the topic of friendship. The following lessons and activities can supplement materials you may already have and will provide further opportunities for allowing children to explore and practice relationship skills. This unit is organized in five parts:

1: Developing Strong Friendship Skills: Making a Friend

2: How to Be the Best Friend You Can Be

3: So Many Different Kinds of Friends

4: Understanding Emotions: Walk in Someone Else's Shoes

5: Structuring Your Classroom to Support Friendships

## 1 Developing Strong Friendship Skills: Making a Friend

Making friends is a subject that deserves much attention. Some of us find it simple to approach others but many people, young and old, find meeting new people to be fraught with difficulty. The books recommended in the Literature Links box provide a wonderful introduction to this topic.

> **Literature Links:**
> *How do I Feel About . . . Making Friends* by Sarah Levete (Copper Beech Books, 1998)
> For third grade: *How Kids Make Friends . . . Secrets for Making Lots of Friends, No Matter How Shy You Are* by Lonnie Michelle (Freedom Press, 1995)

*How Do I Feel About . . . Making Friends* is written in an interview format, with kids speaking as the experts. The author asks these children questions about different facets of friendship, including why friends are important, how they make friends, different kinds of friendships, and keeping friend-ships going. These questions are great jumping-off points for many class-room activities.

*How Kids Make Friends* is a great basic resource for older students and could certainly be adapted for use in younger grades. In kid-friendly language, it spells out, step by step, how to make and keep friends.

After you've read aloud one or both books, encourage students to think about how they might approach a potential friend. Talk about how our body language affects how others see us. Demonstrate, without speaking, various emotions. (Remember, be dramatic! This should be enjoyable for all of you.) Have children identify specific gestures and expressions you use that might show a person that you like him or her and want to be friends. Remind children how smiling, looking people in the eye, standing with a confident posture, and having a cheerful facial expression may help a potential friend warm up to them.

Group children in pairs and have them practice approaching their partner as if he or she were a new friend and, without words, showing their partner that they'd like to be friends. For contrast, you might have them demonstrate nonverbal ways to show an unfriendly approach.

Next, on chart paper, make two columns. In the first, brainstorm things children could say that would be positive ways of introducing themselves to a new friend. Is it enough just to tell the person your name? Does your tone of voice make a difference? Some examples of positive approaches are suggesting to the new friend some sort of activity that you both could do (this gets you both talking and enjoying the time you are spending together) and compli-menting him or her (as long as the compliment is honestly meant).

In the second column, have students think of negative examples. Ask guiding questions such as "Does it help if you are bossy, or demand that the person do something you want to do? Is it better to be loud and pushy, or quieter and respectful?" Take lots of time to come up with ideas and compare them. A second-grade chart is shown at right.

Have students choose a new partner and this time practice introducing them-selves to a new friend, using friendly body language and other positive strategies you've discussed.

| Positive Ways to Make a Friend | Not-So-Good Ways to Make a Friend |
|---|---|
| • Smile, look the person in the eye | • Look grumpy, look over the person's shoulder or at the ground |
| • Say hi, say your name | • Don't tell him or her your name |
| • Ask if he or she wants to play a game | • Tell the person that he or she has to play with you |
| • Ask for his or her name | • Ignore the person when he or she is talking |
| • Tell the person something you like about him or her | • Push the person |
| | • Run away without saying good-bye |

**CHAPTER 6**

You may want to find an open space such as the gym and allow children to practice with all of their classmates, as they rotate around the room. This activity can be a little noisy but children enjoy the opportunity to introduce themselves to all of their classmates, including you. They also benefit from repeated practice.

## EXCLUSIVE AND INCLUSIVE BEHAVIORS

Another important strategy to teach children is how to behave when someone comes over to introduce him- or herself. Spend some time discussing how important it is to appropriately respond to new people. First impressions count!

Brainstorm and list on chart paper things students might say when a new person introduces him- or herself. Body language is very important here, too. Some additional modeling or role-playing will help children evaluate effective responses. Use many different scenarios: meeting someone on the playground, meeting a new student, meeting a friend of your parents, or meeting a visitor to your school. For example, you might describe the following dilemma: If Matt is already playing with other people and a new friend comes over to introduce himself, can Matt just say no or ignore him and run off to play? What should he say? What should he do?

A common issue for children is having more than one friend or friends outside a small circle. Challenge students to suggest friendly ways of handling a situation:

> *If someone asks you to play, how should you handle it if you already are playing with other people? If someone you don't like wants to be friends, how should you handle that?*

Once you have introduced strategies for approaching and welcoming new friends, it is a good time to let children know that while no one can force them to be a friend, everyone must be treated with kindness and respect. You may want to list possible responses to the example situation with Matt above.

*You may want to add a new rule to your class rules list: No one should be excluded from games or other school activities.*

It's important for students to understand that they have a responsibility to include people in games or activities, especially new students. This is a perfect time to ask students to empathize with another person's feelings: Imagine how it would feel to be standing by yourself on the sidelines as the other children played soccer. How would it feel if someone asked you to join? How would you feel if the other children got a birthday party invitation but you didn't? What if you received three valentines at your class party, and others had lots? How would you feel if no one chose you to be on their team for baseball?

Have older students write a short story or a cartoon strip describing a time when someone was excluded and then included. Have younger children create paper-bag puppets and use them to practice various scenarios discussed in class.

## 2 How to Be the Best Friend You Can Be

This lesson helps children see that friendship is a work in progress and they are the architects. Read aloud Loreen Leedy's *How Humans Make Friends*—a humorous take on the work of being a good friend. Zork Tripork, an alien, is reporting on his observations from his trip to planet Earth. His speech is called "How Humans Make Friends" and features specific examples of how friends meet and greet each other, things they do together, what friends talk about, how they get along, why friends don't get along, and how friends solve conflicts.

> **Literature Link:**
>
> *How Humans Make Friends* by Loreen Leedy (Holiday House, 1996)

The sections on how friends get along versus how they don't get along are worth rereading. Zork mentions such things as "Friends can be trusted, friends share, friends are fair, they help each other, and friends keep promises." He is just as specific talking about why friends don't get along (blabbing secrets, teasing, being selfish, acting bossy, breaking promises, acting rude).

Many children will have experienced both kinds of behavior. After you've read the book aloud, encourage children to write or draw their experiences and compile these in a class book. You might choose to use a pattern following the "Fortunately, Unfortunately" format (*Fortunately*, there was a girl who looked friendly; *unfortunately*, she was moving away on Monday). Or change it to a "Friendly, Unfriendly" pattern (He was *friendly* when he offered me his chocolate bar; he was *unfriendly* when he stole my hat). Children's examples make great resources for peers who are struggling; keep this book in your classroom library.

You might share the class book aloud before beginning the next activity, which extends the themes of working together and getting along by providing a visual reminder of how children in your class demonstrate kindness and friendship. Children are motivated and excited when they see their efforts recognized as they work together to create a "friendship chain."

### CREATE A FRIENDSHIP CHAIN

Using anonymous scenarios, give students some examples of the different ways you have seen children being good friends to others. Let them know that you are keeping an eye out for friendly behavior in your room. Can they spot it, too? Challenge children to become "good friend" detectives and build a paper chain of kind deeds that will be as long as the hallway (or your room, or the gym!). The chain can be attached to the ceiling or simply taped onto a wall.

To prepare, cut construction paper strips and put them in an easily accessible spot in the classroom. Give each child one strip to get the chain started. Invite children to write either a good experience they've had being a friend or an example of how friends treat each other with kindness. They can link their circle to the one before, attaching the ends of their strip together with glue or tape.

Hold up the growing chain and tell children that whenever they see someone being a good friend, or experience someone's kindness, they can add a link to the chain by taking a strip and writing down what they observed. Have younger children write their name and the name of the person involved (and if there is time have them draw a picture of what they saw). Have older children write a summary of what happened. You may want the "good friend" to sign the strip as well to acknowledge his or her participation.

These strips can be added as they are written or you may wish to collect them and then spend some time as a class creating the chain. Be careful not to publicize how many links each child has; this is not a personal competition but a class challenge. No one should be put on the spot because they don't have many strips. It is worthwhile at various points throughout the day or week to focus briefly on the chain and read aloud some of the friendly behaviors that children have observed.

You may choose to revisit this activity throughout the year, and vary the format. Use small paper squares instead of links to cover a certain area (for example, you might create a "friendly behavior door"). Use colored interlocking blocks each representing an act of kindness to create a "tower of kindness" (you might tape the tower to a wall with masking tape so it doesn't fall over!).

## 3 So Many Different Kinds of Friends

The focus of this lesson is to help children distinguish between different types of friends. Children often place a high priority on having a "best" friend—often to the exclusion of other relationships. You can offer them models of different kinds of friendships that can be just as satisfying.

On chart paper, list different types of friendships. Gather students for a class discussion and give them a few examples of the different types of friends you have: some who are people you see only once a year, some who have moved away, some who are different ages. You might choose to introduce the word *acquaintance.* To help students with this concept, have them discuss with a peer three differences between acquaintances and best friends.

Ask guiding questions such as "Can brothers and sisters be friends? Do you have friends who are older or younger than you? Do you always have to play if you are friends? Are there other things people can do when they are friends?"

> **Literature Link:**
> *Pinky and Rex and the Bully* by James Howe (Atheneum, 1996)
> *B-E-S-T Friends* by Patricia Reilly Griff (Bantam Doubleday, 1988)

Read aloud *Pinky and Rex and the Bully.* Mrs. Morgan, Rex's next-door neighbor, becomes a good friend to Rex. Relate the things Mrs. Morgan does to the characteristics of being a good friend from the previous activity.

Ask children, "Should you not be friends with someone because he or she is different from you?" This leads to a worthwhile discussion about tolerance, accepting people, and realizing that anyone can be a friend as long as that person makes you feel happy, comfortable, and safe.

Follow up with another read aloud, *B-E-S-T Friends,* a story that models tolerance and empathy in a new friendship. In the story, Stacey is asked to help a new girl, Annie, who is very different and causes problems because of her behavior. Stacey and Annie experience conflict, but unlike her classmates, Stacey recognizes that Annie is an interesting girl in spite of her behavior. She empathizes with Annie and by the end of the story, they become friends.

This discussion also relates to the activity Boring! in Chapter 3. In fact, doing activities that highlight individuality during this lesson will help underscore the idea that we are all unique and have special qualities that help make us good friends to others—being different can help friendships grow.

> Learning about different types of friendships is a great opportunity to get your class involved in the community. Seniors residences are always looking for volunteers or children to come in and spend some time. Many activities relating to your curriculum can be utilized to create a successful "Grandparent" program. Listening to a child read, reminiscing about their lives as a child, and making a craft together are all excellent ways to encourage intergenerational friendships.

Part of being able to accept new friends who are different from ourselves is learning more about the people we meet, just as Stacey does in the story. As a group, discuss the kinds of things that friends like to know about each other. List a few questions that students might ask a partner to get to know him or her better. Draw simple pictures or list words to help younger children remember what to ask.

Have students draw the name of a classmate from a hat, or let them pick the name of a "buddy" in another class. (These partnerships may last for only this activity or be arranged for a longer term.)

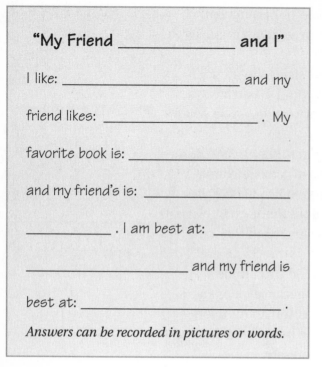

> **"My Friend _____ and I"**
>
> I like: _____ and my
>
> friend likes: _____ . My
>
> favorite book is: _____
>
> and my friend's is: _____
>
> _____ . I am best at: _____
>
> _____ and my friend is
>
> best at: _____ .
>
> *Answers can be recorded in pictures or words.*

When children are paired with a new person —and the goal here is to have each child paired with someone he or she doesn't really know— have them "interview" one another. They could write the answers to four or five prepared questions or fill in a sheet like the sample shown here.

After partners get to know one another, choose an art activity that requires children to work together (for example, take a picture of the partners and then have them create a cardboard or clay picture frame for the result; have partners do a simple cooking activity and then share the results; or have partners make friendship bracelets). These projects help create a bond between participants and may set the stage for a new friendship.

You might choose to end the activity with songs or a story about friendship.

## 4 Understanding Emotions: Walk in Someone Else's Shoes

Feeling empathy for others is a cornerstone of successful relationships. Not surprisingly, one of the skills that children who bully struggle with is empathizing with others. Providing children with opportunities to consider how others feel helps them understand how their actions and reactions can affect another person's feelings.

The three guiding questions that students should always ask themselves are:

*How is that person feeling?*

*How can I tell how he or she is feeling?*

*How would I feel if that happened to me?*

By using this framework consistently, and in many different situations, students begin to internalize these questions and consider the feelings of other people in their lives. The two activities that follow give students practice empathizing.

### I CAN PICTURE WHAT YOU'RE FEELING

If you've already done the second activity from Chapter 5 (page 64), review the emotions vocabulary on the zippy word charts. One way to begin is to have students create a collage of feelings. Remind children of your discussions about making new friends and the importance of body language. Body language gives a lot of information about how others are feeling, and properly "reading" someone's non-verbal communication is an essential skill.

To begin this "reading" lesson, your students will create an "I Know What You're Feeling" collage using pictures from magazines, flyers, and old calendars. Have each student create his or her own piece of art or have the class work on a giant collage. Challenge children to find as many examples of different emotions as they can. Have older students write the appropriate feeling on the bottom of each part of the collage. This could easily be extended into a language arts lesson, introducing synonyms, antonyms, verbs, nouns, and other vocabulary that vividly describe emotions.

By looking for as many examples of facial expressions or body postures as possible, your students will expand their awareness of this universal language. In fact, it's a great opportunity to stress that although people come from different cultures and/or countries, we all understand this basic means of communicating.

## FAIRY TALE CHARACTERS

Another simple empathy-building activity is discussing and analyzing storybook characters and their feelings. Read a story such as "Goldilocks and the Three Bears," "Little Red Riding Hood," or "The Three Little Pigs." Before reading, make a list of the major characters on chart paper. (You might give older students their own sheet to complete.) As you read, stop after each major development and, using the three guiding questions on page 80, discuss how each character may be feeling at that point in the story. For example, you might ask how Baby Bear felt when he discovered that someone had eaten his porridge (he was upset) and how children can tell (he whined and cried). Follow up by asking how they would feel in a similar situation, if someone had eaten their lunch.

After finishing, go back and take a look at the major story events. How did the character's feelings affect what happened next in the story? For example, how was Goldilocks feeling after she ate all of Baby Bear's porridge? (She wasn't hungry anymore, but she was still curious so she went into the living room.)

Developing empathy takes time. Use the guiding questions on page 80 when you discuss stories that include characters feelings—particularly in friendships. "Reading between the lines" or asking students to interpret a character's thoughts and motivations through their actions is an integral part of reading comprehension. If students have a difficult time with this, encourage them to role-play scenarios from the story. At times, viewing or enacting a character's body language helps children understand how emotions and actions may affect the next event.

Reading about conflict between story characters or witnessing real-life disagreements among peers gives children an opportunity to empathize with others. Any conflict situation that you and your students deal with must involve an opportunity for all students involved to share their thoughts and feelings. The same guiding questions are used in the Conflict Resolution unit in Chapter 7.

# 5 Structuring Your Classroom Practice to Support Friendships

Developing tolerance, empathy, and respect for others are ongoing themes that support a bully-free classroom. The way you choose to structure your classroom routines helps. Two goals must dominate your planning: to structure activities that give children the satisfaction of helping others and to offer them many opportunities to interact positively with others (including you!) both in your school and in community settings.

Unfortunately, children who bully rarely have people respond to them positively; they may never have had the feeling that their actions resulted in a positive situation for someone else. Bullies need to see how good it feels to help other people and experience the old saying, "Do unto others as they would do unto you."

The following ideas may help set this structure in place.

## I CAUGHT YOU!

. . . doing something good, that is. Often we keep a close eye on our class to spot misbehaviors; however, catching good behavior has an amazing impact on students who often aren't recognized for positive reasons. Using one of the anecdotal record methods discussed in Chapter 2, keep tabs on positive things you see (see pages 27–28).

When you observe kindness in action, respond immediately. Depending on the child, you may wish to mention it casually as students are working. "Wow, thanks to Daniel for lending Sharisse his eraser. That made her feel great, I bet!" or "Shelly, I appreciate the way you let Karen go ahead of you in the drink line because she had the hiccups. That was really kind."

Use this strategy sparingly; I use it to highlight the kind of behaviors that I want to see in the classroom, usually after a class discussion about sharing or taking turns. You may choose not to use student names as you praise these gestures, but the power of hearing themselves applauded for something positive may be the boost some children—especially bullies—need to act in a friendly way again. More often, I quietly approach the student and make the same comment privately, as some children are embarrassed by praise or being in the spotlight for any reason. Again, you really have to know your students to understand the best way to acknowledge their efforts.

My favorite way of recognizing great behavior is to create a note of recognition on the computer and run off a few. Writing a quick note to a student is a wonderful way to communicate. Even younger children can understand "Thank you." Be sure to specifically state what you saw ("You were being a good friend" isn't descriptive enough) and attach a celebratory sticker. Use the reproducible notes on page 83 or create your own.

Casually drop the note on the student's desk or in his or her cubby.

☆ I Caught You . . . Doing Something Terrific!

Dear _____

_____
Your Teacher

☆ I Caught You . . . Doing Something Terrific!

Dear _____

_____
Your Teacher

☆ I Caught You . . . Doing Something Terrific!

Dear _____

_____
Your Teacher

☆ I Caught You . . . Doing Something Terrific!

Dear _____

_____
Your Teacher

**CHAPTER 6**

(My favorite way to deliver a note is to hide it in a shoe or coat pocket when children are out of the room). Children really value these notes; having something in writing is real proof that they did something well. One of the toughest children I worked with pretended to crumple an "I Caught You" note I gave him and throw it away. When no one was looking, he carefully retrieved it, flattened it out, and taped it to the inside of his pencil box where he kept it the rest of the year.

I also use nonverbal signals, especially in public situations when it's not appropriate to give more formal recognition. A wink and a thumbs-up is an effective way to say, "I caught you doing something good!"

## WELCOME TO OUR ROOM!

A challenge throughout the year in many classrooms is the arrival of new students who must be welcomed into the community you and your class have built. It's a great idea, especially at the beginning of the year, to have your class plan and prepare materials to help you welcome new students—the better prepared you are, the smoother the transition will be.

> **Literature Link:**
> *Make New Friends* by Rosemary Wells (Hyperion, 2003)

Begin by reading the book *Make New Friends.* Juanita is a new student and Yoko becomes her guide to settling into their classroom. Yoko is "Captain of the Friend Ship" and helps Juanita in various ways.

Use the Friend Ship theme for your class; have everyone make Captain Hats (traditional paper hats would work), which they can wear on the day a new student arrives. Draw two names from a hat or find another fair way to decide in advance who will be the first "Captains of the Friend Ship" when a new student arrives; these children may help new students get acclimated and make a hat when they arrive.

Have older students create a class handbook, telling about your standards of behavior, class routines, and other important information a new person would need to know. This is a handy activity for children who are "fast-finishers"—they can create extras of these materials to have on hand for new arrivals.

Create a plan for what will happen when a new student arrives. For example, keeping a box of cookies and a few containers of juice on hand means your class could celebrate a new arrival with a treat. Note that these new-arrival activities don't have to hijack your whole day but will contribute to all students feeling that they are a family and create opportunities for new friendships to form.

## SHHHHH! I'M YOUR SECRET PAL

Doing good deeds makes a person feel good about him- or herself; it's important for children to feel the basic satisfaction of helping someone else and develop the intrinsic motivation to do things for others because they want to, not because they must. Doing good deeds in a discreet way increases the enjoyment and allows children to experience the action personally, out of the spotlight. In this activity children plan to do good deeds for someone secretly over the course of one to three days.

Choose another class for your students to buddy with or simply pair children in your classroom. You may choose to assign buddies or allow your students to draw names.

With younger children especially, take time to discuss how to keep a secret (and point out the difference between good secrets and bad ones to keep). I've found that having children sign a "I Can Keep a Secret" pledge poster usually does the trick.

Brainstorm a list of kind things that your students could do for someone else. Don't allow students to bring in gifts from home—focus on the *giving,* not the *gift* aspect. "Giving" ideas might include:

- Drawing a picture for your buddy

- Leaving a complimentary note about your buddy

- Putting something away that belongs to your buddy if he or she forgets

- Leaving a joke on his or her desk

- Helping your buddy if he or she is having trouble with a question (but not telling them you're the secret pal)

If you're partnering with another class, arrange with the other teacher to let your class sneak in when his or her class is out of the room. Secret pals may leave a gift or do something once or twice for their pal. (Make sure you have an extra gift ready to leave in case one of your children is absent.) Encourage students to reflect on how it felt to do something positive for someone else without being rewarded or recognized. Let them write a note to you sharing their feelings.

● ● ●

Friends are so important to all of us. By discussing friendships, having children practice making and keeping friends, and introducing them to the concepts of respect, tolerance, and empathy, we can give children opportunities to feel the satisfaction of being with and caring about others. By carefully structuring our class routines we can help all children—and bullies in particular—feel likeable and successful when dealing with other people.

# Conflict Resolution

## *(The Big Four, Unit Four)*

CHAPTER 7

*This chapter offers management strategies and activities to teach conflict resolution— a problem-solving tool children can use to peacefully settle arguments with peers and to gain the skills and confidence they need to face social challenges like bullies.*

"I'M TELLING!" roared Bill at John, two boys seated in the same group.

"Okay, HERE. Take your stupid pencil. I didn't steal it, I needed it for a few seconds," retorted John.

"You are not a friend of mine anymore, you stealer," said Bill, stalking off.

While the bullying episodes in our classroom had dramatically reduced, the incidence of bickering and difficulties during the day continued to be a headache. Arguments about pencils, cutting into line or who had dibs on the class novel during independent reading time were small irritations that took time out of our day. It seemed expedient for me to jump in and resolve issues so the class could continue its work, but I knew my intervention was at the expense of children becoming responsible problem-solvers themselves.

My students tended not to take ownership for daily disputes that arose or for their resolution. As a result, they were often angry and complained to their peers that they weren't listened to or treated fairly. I also discovered that by not dealing effectively with conflict, I had unwittingly placed timid and passive children, who were reluctant to stand up for themselves, in a vulnerable position to be bullied.

In short, dealing with all kinds of conflict was something my students needed to learn. Our work in bully-proofing helped them understand the difference between bullying behavior and everyday conflict (Chapter 3). Now they deserved explicit instruction in taking ownership of and solving these conflicts with guidance—not with hand-holding from me.

Preparing children to deal with conflict successfully became the final goal of my bully-proofing plan.

In developing my conflict resolution unit, I revisited materials I had collected at peer mediation and other problem-solving workshops and did some more research. I liked what conflict resolution had to offer my students: ownership of solving their problems through a constructive discussion with peers in a safe environment. I began to implement some of the strategies and, through trial and error, developed a simple, struc-tured three-step framework for problem solving that works for primary-grade children.

As part of a bully-proofing plan, teaching conflict resolution has major benefits: it holds children accountable for their behavior and requires restitution. Bullies don't like their behavior to be out in the open, to face their target, or to have to listen to how their actions affected another person. As well, bullies realize that they will be confronted and held responsible for their actions in a conflict resolution classroom.

Vulnerable children, too, benefit immensely from being able to confront their tormentor in a controlled, safe setting. As Carla Garrity writes in *Bully-Proofing Your School,* "Remember, vulnerability attracts aggressors. Helping the students work for small gains that nurture their confidence and strength will be beneficial."

Small gains for children who do not assert themselves effectively are so important. Consider this from a child's perspective: if a classmate takes your pencil and you are able to confront him or her, talk about what he or she did and how you feel about it, and then come to a solution that both of you agree on, you'll feel empowered. Pencil issues are not life-and-death situations, but they allow students the opportunity to feel successful and capable—"I can handle this, and I know what to do."

Children who feel successful and capable solving minor problems are more likely to stand up for themselves and learn to handle conflict appropriately in general. Children who are confident problem solvers are not as intimidated by aggression or threatening behavior of bullies. Rather, they understand the process of addressing the problem with the other student, relying on adults when necessary to act as coaches rather than solvers. They take ownership for the problem and agree to a solution that works for the people involved.

My students invariably have developed such confidence solving problems that by the end of the year most, if not all, problems that developed in the classroom have been dealt with quickly and successfully by the children with little input from me.

The model introduced here is very structured; children are able to practice solving problems, large and small, with others. By following these steps, they become skilled at identifying the main issue, calmly discussing it, and working together to come up with a resolution that is satisfactory to all. As a teacher, you become a coach, not the "resolver/enforcer" of problems in your classroom.

> In classrooms with effective conflict resolution in place, the goal is to enable every child to become comfortable talking out minor, everyday problems and taking ownership of the problem-solving process. However, when serious situations arise that children cannot handle on their own— when they are in danger, feel threatened, or are involved in patterns of bullying behavior— you must intervene.

I begin to introduce conflict resolution the first week of school but as with any other component in this book, you can begin at any time during the school year. This unit takes at least three weeks of daily blocks of time, both to do the activities outlined below and to give students time to practice. Conflict resolution skills must be consistently applied every time there are conflict situations. This will take time at first, but the rewards are huge.

This chapter is organized in five sections dealing with management strategies and activities to teach conflict resolution.

1. Managing Conflict Resolution in the Classroom

2. Introducing Conflict Resolution to Children

3. Helping Children Control Their Emotions

4. A Conflict Resolution Framework

5. Coaching Strategies: Step-by-Step Conflict Resolution

CHAPTER 7

# 1 Managing Conflict Resolution in the Classroom

As discussed in Chapter 2, you may find it helpful to plan a block of time during the day to use for dealing with conflict situations or bullying problems. I prefer to use if necessary the first fifteen minutes after recess and lunch to pull children together to resolve problems; they really do need to be resolved as quickly as possible with younger students.

It pays dividends in classroom harmony and productivity when upset and angry children are able to discuss a problem, resolve it, and then move into other classroom activities smoothly. Of course, some conflicts, especially repeated incidents, may need to be dealt with after school, but it's still necessary to meet as soon as possible with the children involved and then let them know this will happen.

After deciding how conflict resolution will fit into your schedule, the next concern is organizing the classroom so students who are not involved in conflict resolution use this time constructively.

The solution is a list of tasks the students choose independently to work at while you are otherwise occupied. (This management strategy is also helpful for those times when you need a few uninterrupted moments, whether to speak to the principal, tally up the field trip money, or give parent volunteers their work for the day.) The activities need to be simple, quiet, and independent; you want to avoid activities with lots of materials or groups of children taking part in a discussion-based activity when the time will be short. You'll want to resume regular work as soon as the conflict is resolved.

As a class, we come up with a list of activities the other children are to do (and *not* to do) when I am involved in resolving conflicts or otherwise engaged. We list these ideas on poster paper. Some of these ideas, shown below, may work for your class.

## WHEN MY TEACHER IS NOT AVAILABLE . . .

| What *can* I do? | What *can't* I do? |
|---|---|
| • read | • play a math game |
| • play with clay at my desk | • sit and do nothing |
| • finish other work | • talk with friends |
| • do a math tub activity by myself | • play with a toy |
| • do Writer's Workshop | • play with center materials |
| • read quietly with one friend | • read with a group of friends |
| • draw a picture | • paint at the easel |

This is the blueprint for children to follow when you are working with a conflict situation, so it's important to have children practice choosing from this list a few times before you ask them to do this independently. Finding time to practice should be easy to do; there are often times during a school day when you need a break for a few minutes, either to complete paperwork or just to catch your breath.

Clearly state what you expect to happen when you give your class the signal that you are not to be disturbed. Introduce and review the parameters for behavior during conflict resolution; for example, I insist that I am not disturbed unless someone is bleeding, throwing up, or in danger. Bathroom breaks are not a good enough reason to interrupt me.

Introduce children to the signal they should watch or listen for to show that you will be involved in a conflict resolution conference for a few moments. By choosing an interesting or unusual signal, you increase the chances of children cooperating. You could play a scale on a xylophone, clap rhythmically, or wave a colorful scarf—choose a way of attracting their attention that is unique to the conflict resolution situation. One of my favorite attention-grabbers is to put on a lovely hat with a veil left over from Hat Day. This works very well; children love to see me wearing the hat, and it is unusual enough to attract attention.

Give the signal and allow children a minute or so to make a choice and get themselves to work. Remember, these activities should not be intensive or require a lot of time or material; most of the time students will only be doing them for a few short minutes.

Continue to practice a few times a day for a week until children respond quickly and make appropriate activity choices.

## 2 Introducing Conflict Resolution to Children

When you are sure that children are able to make good choices for working independently during conflict resolution time and get themselves on track when necessary, you are ready to introduce the structure for resolving problems. Gather students for a class discussion.

To begin, you may wish to review the differences between conflict and bullying, as discussed in Chapter 3 and refer to the chart "What's the Difference Between Bullying and Conflict?" that you may have created (see page 36).

Emphasize how important it is for children to be able to work out problems with others. Ask:

> *Is it best to always have an adult solve problems for you? Why? If you are angry with someone, would it be a good idea to just ignore that person and not tell him or her how you feel? Why?*

**CHAPTER 7**

Help children identify some behaviors they may already use to solve problems with peers, such as talking out the problem, asking an adult to help, and writing a note to the other person explaining how the problem makes you feel. For contrast, have them list some behaviors that would not help solve a problem, such as crying, yelling, hitting, and saying "I don't care." Emphasize that there are many ways of solving a problem so that everyone involved feels satisfied.

> **Literature Link:**
> *I Want It* by Elizabeth Crary (Parenting Press, 2001)

Read aloud *I Want It*, a story with an engaging format that shows a variety of ways to solve a problem. In the story, Megan and Amy are playing together and a conflict arises when Amy wants to play with a toy that Megan has. Amy considers seven different ways she can get the toy, all with different outcomes. Since it's written in a "story tree" format, the readers make the decisions and see the consequences of each choice.

The book includes helpful questions about feelings and making decisions as each alternative is considered. It's designed to be read with a teacher or parent and the pages in the back summarize and evaluate the ideas and choices presented.

This book also gives you the opportunity to discuss the angry or hurt feelings people may have when they don't like the way someone else has treated them. It's important to stress that these feelings are all normal, but it is how a person handles those feelings that count. You might select short passages from other books you've read together in which characters either show a strong or a controlled reaction to a problem they face. Ask students to identify which characters were most successful in dealing with their problem effectively—the examples should help children consider which is the better way to resolve a problem. They will have the opportunity to gauge their own responses in the next activity.

## 3 Helping Children Control Their Emotions

Anger is the one emotion that most children automatically associate with conflict. Allow time to have children share how they express anger and point out how it can build. Ask children to identify strategies they use to calm down and gain control over their emotions.

"The Anger Escalator" developed by Beth Teolis in *Ready to Use Conflict Resolution Activities* (1998) offers a helpful image for students to use when they are angry. With a simple drawing on the chalkboard, point out the way escalators carry people up and down. Have children picture a person getting angrier and angrier as someone riding an "anger escalator." Ask them what happens as the person goes up with each step?

Have them share with a partner how they feel as they get angry—what happens to their body language? their voices? the way they act?

Now have them think about how they can bring themselves down the "anger escalator." You might share some of your own strategies first or suggest strategies you'd like them to try—taking a deep breath, counting to ten, consciously clenching and relaxing your fists, and saying something reassuring to yourself are all good ways for children to begin to bring the emotion under control. You could certainly refer students to the "Breathe Deep!" strategy they may have listed in their Power Books (see Chapter 4).

Have older students create an "anger escalator" poster that illustrates the feelings they experience when their anger builds, and the strategies they use to calm themselves. Draw a simple step organizer and have students copy it onto a sheet of construction paper (make copies for younger students). Have students write or draw three or four stages of getting angry and calming down in this format. This same elevator example can be used to chart other emotions, such as fear or excitement. The illustration below shows a simple way to chart the process of getting angry.

Some students have particular difficulty calming themselves, whether they are excited or upset. Teaching effective strategies and having students use the escalator image encourages children to take responsibility for their emotions. Remember, the goal here is not to eliminate the feeling, just to help control it. Reassure children that emotions are normal and often help us communicate with others. It's how we handle our emotions that can help us solve our problems in ways that make us feel good about ourselves and our relationships.

# 4 A Conflict Resolution Framework

Now that you have introduced children to the concept of anger management and stated the expectation that they resolve small problems independently, you're ready to introduce the conflict resolution model. In a class discussion, define conflict resolution as a way people can solve problems with others by talking it out and coming to a solution everyone agrees on.

> Conflict resolution is a way children can talk out problems with others. In conflict resolution, each child has the chance to tell his or her side of the story and how it made him or her feel, and with the teacher's help, decide how to solve the problem.

## CONFLICT RESOLUTION CHECKLIST

**To solve a problem, we will:**

- tell our teacher we need to resolve a problem.

- use our "My Turn" statements to give each person a chance to tell their side of the story.

- decide on a solution that is fair for both people.

- shake hands. The problem is solved.

On poster paper, develop a checklist showing the steps everyone will follow when solving a problem using the conflict resolution model. Use the checklist at left as a guideline and hang the poster in a prominent spot in your room.

Students need to understand that you will not allow them to simply complain about a problem they are having with someone; all parties involved must be included from the beginning. This may be a good time to reiterate the difference between tattling and telling, as described in Chapter 4. If a child comes to me and begins to complain about another child's behavior, I ask him or her to think about whether this is tattling or telling. I remind the child that if he or she has a problem to work out with someone, that person needs to be involved. Never allow a child to pour out his or her story before the other child involved in the conflict has joined you.

After you've reviewed the checklist with your class, introduce the "my turn to talk" statements that the children will use in every problem-solving situation. These statements are highlighted in bold in the box at left and follow the prompts you will use with each child. Post them next to the checklist poster.

## MY TURN TO TALK

What will you say when you are problem solving?

1. Tell _____ what the problem is.

   **The problem is that . . .**

2. Tell _____ how that made you feel. (How do you think it made the other person feel?)

   **That made me feel . . .**

3. Tell _____ what you want him or her to do next time.

   **Next time, I want you to . . .**

Show children this model in action. You might recruit a few trusted older students who are good problem solvers, review the conflict resolution model with them, and give them a scenario to practice, so they can perform for your class. I ask former students to come in and role-play conflict resolution situations. This works for two reasons: it allows my former students to shine and their message resonates strongly with their younger audience.

To prepare, have your class brainstorm some common conflicts they encounter with peers. Using the list of ideas, have your volunteer actors go through the steps to resolve the problems.

You may wish to have your actors come in for a few minutes every day for a week to demonstrate; they could be asked to act out and resolve actual problems that have occurred that day. Be sure to remind children that problems can have more than one good solution.

As your volunteer actors demonstrate the process, be sure to draw children's attention to their body language and behavior as they talk out the problem. Body language can play a big role in successful problem solving. You may choose to have the volunteers act out some unhelpful behavior for contrast and show that looking at the floor, mumbling, slouching, crossing their arms, or yelling at someone negatively affects how the problem is solved.

Make your body language and behavior expectations for conflict resolution very clear. These should be listed on a separate sheet of chart paper (see sample, right).

Be sure children understand that the last rule means that you and their classmates expect them to deal with a conflict situation cooperatively and honestly. Children who use the phrase "I don't know" are copping out; you might role-play an example of how "I don't know" can effectively roadblock any attempt to solve a problem.

> ## CONFLICT RESOLUTION TALKING TIPS
>
> ### When you are talking out a problem:
>
> - Look at the other person's face and into his or her eyes.
>
> - Speak in a calm, clear voice. Don't mumble.
>
> - Stand up straight and face the other person.
>
> - Try your best: "I don't know" is not allowed.

In fact, the basic body language "rules" listed in the box above work any time people communicate with one another. Seek opportunities to reinforce these rules whenever children speak with you or one another.

To wrap up this lesson, have younger students illustrate a prepared booklet with each of the behavior expectations written at the bottom of each page. Have older students create a rap or skipping chant, or write a story contrasting effective and ineffective ways of solving a problem with another person.

## GUIDING CHILDREN THROUGH THE PROCESS

Your job during conflict resolution time is to act as a coach, asking the guiding questions and keeping the discussion on track. Following is a conflict resolution dialogue I had with two students over the issue of a pencil taken without permission. My goals are to focus the discussion, keep the children on track, and help them generate solutions to the problem.

Read the dialogue and then review how to coach children through a conflict resolution session, step by step, on pages 95–97.

**SAMPLE OF CONFLICT-RESOLUTION DIALOGUE**

*Bill:* Mrs. M, John and I have a problem.

*Mrs. M:* Okay, I'll put my hat on.

*John:* I already told you I won't take it again.

*Mrs. M:* John, our rule is that you two need to do some conflict resolution with me. Bill, please tell John what the problem is.

*Bill:* The problem is that you stole my pencil and you just took it off my desk without even asking me.

*John:* I couldn't because—

*Mrs. M:* John, it's Bill's turn to talk. You need to listen right now. Bill, tell John how that made you feel.

*Bill:* I felt … *(pauses to look at a "zippy words" list) furious* because you didn't even ask me, you just took it. And it hurt my feelings, too.

*Mrs. M:* Tell John what you want him to do next time.

*Bill:* Next time I want you to ask me before you take it and not steal it.

*Mrs. M:* John, tell Bill about this problem.

*John:* Well, I needed a pencil and you said I could use it last week and I couldn't ask you 'cause you took so long in the bathroom and I only used it for a minute but I forgot to give it back and I never stole it.

*Mrs. M:* John, how did you feel when you took his pencil.

*John:* Okay, because I was only borrowing it. If I was really stealing it I would feel mad.

*Mrs. M:* John, how do you think Bill felt?

*John:* Well, angry at me, I guess.

*Mrs. M:* Tell Bill what you will do next time.

*John:* I won't take your pencil, I'll wait for you to come back.

*Mrs. M:* Are there any other choices you could make next time?

*John:* I guess I could use a colored pencil to do my work.

*Mrs. M:* Hmmm, in our class you can't use colored pencils for your work. What about asking someone else sitting in your group for a pencil? Or could you look in your desk or on the floor to find your own pencil? Could you check the spare pencil box on my desk?

*John:* Yeah, I could ask someone else in my group. That's what I'll do next time

*Mrs. M:* Bill, do you have your pencil back?

*Bill:* Yep.

*Mrs. M:* Is the problem solved? Are you friends again?

*John and Bill:* Yeah, friends again.

*Mrs. M:* Okay, shake on it, and John, please remind us what you will do next time.

*John (shaking hands):* Sorry, Bill. Next time I will ask you or somebody else.

*Mrs. M:* Great job. Problem solved, let's get back to work.

# 5 Coaching Strategies: Step-by-Step Conflict Resolution

When time is of the essence and emotions are running high, you'll appreciate having a structured approach that students know well and that you can follow in every situation. This three-step framework helps you and the children involved stay focused and calm and find a solution. Each step is outlined below and uses as an example the model conflict resolution dialogue included on page 94.

## STEP ONE: Set the Stage

**Have students let you know there is a problem to be resolved.** I insist that even if a different teacher has dealt with a problem, the children still go through the steps with me so I can ensure they are following the process through successfully. This is especially true if the other teacher does not follow the conflict resolution model.

When you have gathered together the children involved in the conflict, make sure they are calm enough to resolve the problem. There's no point in going through the process if someone is extremely upset or crying. If emotions are running high, ask both children to go to separate areas for a few minutes until they are ready to calmly talk out the problem. A reminder to use their "anger escalator" strategies to calm themselves down may help (see pages 90–91). Some children have great difficulty settling themselves down, but they learn quickly when they are in a "time out" situation and are not receiving any attention or interest that may fuel their emotions.

Children settle down quickly when they know that they will have equal time to share their side of the story and their feelings.

Insist on fair and equal opportunities for children to speak and be heard. This is an essential part of the conflict resolution process; everyone involved is given the courtesy of being heard, and no one is allowed to interrupt or shortchange someone when it's another person's turn to speak. When children interrupt, remind them that they will have their chance to speak; now it's time for them to really listen to the other side of the story. You may find it helpful to have an object for students to hold when it's their turn to speak. "Peace feathers" (paper cut-out feathers), a small beanbag, or foam balls are all excellent choices (make sure they're soft, just in case someone loses his or her temper). As a last resort, ask a child who interrupts frequently to put a finger over his or her lips while the other person is speaking.

*Refer to the My Turn to Talk prompt poster you've created to guide you and your students through a conflict resolution dialogue. (see page 92).*

## STEP TWO: Use the "My Turn to Talk" Prompts

The child with the grievance begins the conflict resolution session.

CHAPTER 7

*Prompt the child, **"Tell John what the problem is."** Then have the child repeat the sentence and describe the problem.*

**"The problem is that you stole my pencil and you just took it off my desk without even asking me."**

When you first begin conflict resolution with your class, children may look at you and tell you what happened. Gently remind them that you didn't cause their problem; they need to remember the behavior expectations and talk to the child they have the problem with. Some children have great difficulty facing a peer with their complaint, but by allowing them to complain to you, you are in effect, setting yourself up as the judge, not the coach. Sometimes reviewing the Conflict Resolution Talking Tips chart is necessary (see page 93).

Do not accept a statement that is vague. "You were being mean to me" tells the other child nothing about the problem.

*Ask the child to be specific: **"Tell John exactly what he did that is a problem for you."** A clear statement identifies the problem.*

**"You stole my pencil and you just took it off my desk without even asking me."**

*Prompt the child to share his or her feelings: **"Tell John how that made you feel."***

**"I felt furious because you didn't even ask me, you just took it. And that hurt my feelings, too."**

Some children have real difficulty articulating how they feel and this is where your "zippy words" are very helpful (see Chapter 3). Encourage children to find a word that really describes how they feel. Give children "think" time; allow at least 10 seconds of silence to give children a chance to organize their thoughts. You may need to guide a word choice, which is fine, and remind them that it's possible to feel more than one emotion at a time.

*Finally, encourage the child: **"Tell John what you want him to do next time."** This is a great way to have children think about solutions and restitution if necessary.*

Now it's the other child's turn and he or she goes through the same three "My turn to talk" prompts listed on the chart paper. This gives the other child involved the chance to tell his or her side of the story and express his or her feelings. The second question should include the child's feelings about what he or she did and how the action affected the other child: **"John, how did you feel when you took his pencil? How do you**

**think Bill felt?"** These questions are essential to helping students develop empathy.

The response from the second child can often be quite revealing; it's not unusual for the accused child to be reacting to a grievance he or she had about a previous incident. For example, a variation of this situation could be that John took Bill's pencil because Bill took his eraser without asking. Discovering this information allows you to have students deal with both issues. Help children see that not dealing with small problems can lead to bigger ones.

### STEP THREE: Help Students Find and Agree on a Solution

Agreeing upon a solution that works for both students is the last step. Often children know what to do and come up readily with ideas.

Apologies are necessary, along with a statement about what the offender will do the next time. "**Sorry, Bill. Next time I will ask you or somebody else**" is all that's necessary.

If students have difficulty coming up with a solution, lay out various ways they can resolve a problem and then have them agree on the one they feel will work.

Resist the urge to direct children's decisions; you are simply there to help provide choices if necessary. Notice how the final sentence in this response plays on the teacher's role as expert: "**What about asking someone else sitting in your group for a pencil? Or could you look in your desk or on the floor to find your own pencil? Could you check the spare pencil box on my desk?** *Of course, the easiest thing to do would be to apologize and promise not to take anything off his desk without asking again.*"

It's easy to unwittingly signal your preference but it's not up to you to decide what's best for children in a problem they can handle. The final outcome will be one you can live with if all the options you offer are within the bounds of your standards of behavior.

When both children are comfortable with the solution, I will often "hit the rewind button!" so they can act out the original problem with the new solution. I push a spot on their foreheads, make a whirring sound, and then say, "Try again." The children reenact the original problem, this time solving the conflict the way they have agreed upon. Kids love this step and it's a quick indicator of whether they've understood the problem and can demonstrate how they will handle it next time. Usually this ends in smiles, which is a nice way to lead into the last gesture, shaking hands.

After children shake hands, the situation is resolved and isn't referred to again in class. You may want to keep an anecdotal record of each problem solved in a conflict resolution meeting. Such notes may prove helpful in parent conferences and for documenting a pattern if a student repeatedly exhibits a problematic behavior.

**CHAPTER 7**

## THE BENEFITS OF MAKING CONFLICT RESOLUTION A CLASSROOM PRACTICE

Though the conflict resolution process takes focus and practice, children quickly learn the steps to solving a problem with peers, and after one or two meetings, conflict resolution rarely takes more than five minutes from start to finish. That small amount of time results in huge rewards for your students. Confident, capable problem solvers tend not to be the targets of bullies, and conflict resolution offers benefits to bullies themselves.

Expected to assume responsibility for their behavior, students who bully may learn to recognize and experience the feelings of others and learn to empathize through this process. The conflict resolution model also holds them accountable for making amends and provides an opportunity to think about and practice more acceptable behavior in the future. Further, they may experience a positive feeling when their apology is accepted. Laughter and a handshake go a long way toward making everyone feel equal and valued.

Children who are bullied are exposed to an excellent modeling process as they learn to express themselves assertively and take part in coming up with a satisfactory resolution in a safe, supportive environment.

As an extension to your classroom practice, you may choose to share this method with your students' parents. Many parents are always looking for new ideas to use at home, especially when there are siblings, and having parents try this at home supports your program.

During a Parent-Teacher Night, you might want to give an overview of the process, including a detailed handout using the same conflict resolution steps and vocabulary that you use in the classroom. Sessions can be held after school, at lunchtime, or in the evening. I have held successful mini-workshops for parents, following the same basic steps I follow when I introduce conflict resolution to students. I've found that inviting parents for a short workshop before a regularly scheduled parent–school council meeting ensured that I had a good turnout and the following meeting set a clear time limit.

Parents who use the conflict resolution model at home frequently are impressed by their children's ability to solve problems independently. Once you can extend the conflict resolution model to parents, you can often make a case for involving the community at large in a full bully-proofing plan.

• • •

The next chapter will explore how to implement a successful bully-proofing program throughout a school setting.

Creating a Bully-Free Classroom • Scholastic Teaching Resources

# Working Toward a Bully-Free School

*This chapter provides suggestions for involving your school's administration to expand a classroom bully-free plan to a school-wide program that also addresses the concerns of parents and students in the larger community.*

As a veteran teacher, I've taught at many schools. The one thing I've always looked for as I met the principals and staff was how they related and responded to the children in the school.

One of the best schools I ever taught in was a place where children were genuinely valued and cared for. The first day I walked in to meet the staff, I encountered my new principal, Don, in the hallway. He was surrounded by children, all laughing, telling jokes, and trying to get his attention. He had two kindergarten children literally hanging onto one leg while he helped a sixth grader adjust his backpack straps and shared his latest "Riddle of the Day" with a child who had missed the announcements earlier that morning. The feeling of happiness, respect, caring, and warmth that Don embodied also characterized that school, its policies, and discipline methods. Wonderful things happened there because of Don's example and leadership.

The school I was unhappiest in, and almost left teaching because of, was a place where the administrative team was divorced from the life of the students. When he walked in the hallways, the principal rarely acknowledged students or teachers. Neither were valued. His example of poor leadership impacted the structure and well being of the entire school. Comments in staff meetings indicated that students were often an impediment to the smooth, efficient running of a school. Most upsetting to me as a new teacher was that many staff members seemed to be uninterested in their work with children; most had been at the school a long time and were unwilling or unable to muster much enthusiasm for new ideas or ways of doing things. I felt just as excluded and unhappy as many of the students. Not surprisingly, the school was rife with incidents of bullying and disrespectful behavior toward other students and staff. Discipline problems ballooned through the year.

My brief experience in this dispiriting place—and my many years in very different school environments where administrators were dedicated to the social well-being of students and staff—have served as a constant reminder to me that administrators set the tone for the school, and it is their leadership and vision that can make or break a school. A wise administrator leads the way in creating a healthy, productive school life for children. Such an environment can make a huge difference in mitigating conflicts among students and bullying in particular.

This chapter provides suggestions for involving your school's administration to expand a classroom bully-free plan to a school-wide program that also addresses the concerns of parents and students in the broader community. The eight areas it covers include:

1. Administrators Lead the Way

2. Getting Started: Assessing Your School's Bullying Policy

## 1 Administrators Lead the Way

You know your school is ready to begin a new program when your administrators are fully behind it. An effective administration recognizes the need for school-wide policies and commits to making sure the school's organization and rules support this goal. For teachers to "buy into" this vision, they must believe that the principal and the administrative team understand the realities of classrooms today. Policies need to be designed with an understanding of the situation that exists for each person involved. The goal must be to develop realistic, "do-able" strategies instead of policies that are either too theoretical and/or not practical. If a policy is too time-consuming or unrealistic, no one will follow it.

However, administrators shouldn't be expected to construct these guidelines by themselves; discussion and feedback from teachers, students, and parents are essential. Guidelines for gathering and using community feedback on policies that deal with bullying follow. However, the final parameters of any policy rest with the principal and must be consistently and absolutely followed by each staff member.

## 2 Getting Started: Assessing Your School's Bullying Policy

Setting a zero-tolerance policy for bullying is a goal of many schools these days. However, before your principal and staff can articulate that policy clearly, there must be many opportunities for open, honest discussion about what takes place in classrooms, on the playground, in the lunchroom, and on the school bus. Too often, administrators don't fully understand the impact of bullying in a classroom and may be surprised to hear about the depth of the problem that exists in their school.

Chapter 2 prompted you to examine your personal beliefs and current strategies—taking an honest assessment of how bullying myths and personal attitudes affect how you deal with bullies and bullied children in your classroom. This is also a good place to begin when devising school-wide policies about bullying. Led by the administrative team, staff members must first assess how your school currently deals with bullies. In short, what is your school doing right and where are the gaps?

Developing a new framework and strategies for dealing with bullying doesn't happen overnight. Let these questions form the basis of both formal and informal discussions with your staff. It is important for teachers and support staff to have input and help the administrative team understand their motivations and feelings. Principals don't have all the answers and the staff members on the "front line" often have very sensible strategies or ideas that they believe can help with this issue.

It's also very important to urge everyone to look beyond what's always been done and examine the problem from a new perspective. Just because bullying has always involved a detention doesn't necessarily mean that this is the most effective way of dealing with a bully. Encourage creativity over tradition. For example, being proactive with bullies and involving them with a mentor may be a very effective way of preempting a problem before it begins.

As with any guiding principle, building a bully-proofing policy around a set of standards that everyone agrees on is critical. When your staff has developed a clear stand on bullying, the first step to ensuring that all children get the same message about behavior expectations is developing school-wide standards of behavior. When the staff has agreed on these, each teacher can use them as a guide to create his or her own class standards.

A school's standards of behavior might include basic expectations that revolve around the "Big Three" themes—respect, tolerance, and empathy. (See box at right.) These themes will be

> **THE GUIDING QUESTIONS YOU MIGHT CONSIDER INCLUDE:**
> - Does your school have a policy on bullying in place?
> - What guidelines are in place now, and are there a clear series of steps teachers can follow when dealing with repeated bullying situations?
> - Is the current policy based on a well-thought-out philosophy or simply in place because bullying has always been handled a certain way?
> - When does the administration team become involved in bullying situations?
> - How are students monitored when they've been involved in bullying incidents?
> - Does any form of documentation exist to achieve this?
> - Have parents been informed about this school policy?
> - What consequences appear to be successful with students?

> ## SCHOOL-WIDE STANDARDS OF BEHAVIOR
>
> We treat everyone with respect in our school. (Respect)
>
> Everyone will be treated fairly and with kindness, no matter who they are. (Tolerance)
>
> We think about other people's thoughts and feelings and how our actions may affect others. (Empathy)

**CHAPTER 8**

reflected in the guidelines you create, the rules you will ask students to follow and the consequences you and your staff deem acceptable. The Big Three form the bedrock on which all of the other policies on bullying are built and they should be non-negotiable.

## 3 Involving Students and Parents

Getting parents and students involved in this process is very important, but it's a step that must be carefully handled. Your school can gather information from parents and students in many ways, including class meetings, parent-teacher conferences or Open House nights, Parent-Teacher Association meetings, suggestion boxes, and surveys.

Well-designed school-wide surveys, like the one shown here, can be helpful but must be constructed very carefully to ensure that the information you receive is useful and doesn't become an opportunity for people to vent or share their bad experiences or unrealistic expectations. The focus must be on looking ahead, not the mistakes or problems of the past. To facilitate focused feedback, include an introduction in the survey that outlines for parents and students the bully-free mission and the standards of behavior your staff has discussed. Then include only those questions you really need to have answered. Too often, if there are no clear guidelines in place, the volume and strong opinions of some parents in particular can be difficult to incorporate in a policy that will work for all students and staff. A clear, well-planned

---

### Sample Survey About Bullying (for Parents and Students)

This year at P— Elementary, our school community is actively dealing with the problem of student bullying. This focus relates to our school-wide **standards of behavior** (discussed in the first newsletter):

> **Treat everyone with respect.**
> **Don't do anything to others that you wouldn't want done to you.**
> **Everyone must feel safe in our classroom.**

At upcoming parent-teacher meetings, as well as our Parent-School Associations gatherings, we look forward to sharing our school philosophy and our action plans with you.

To give us a clear picture of student and parent perspectives on our current school policies regarding bullying, we ask that you and your child take a few moments to fill out this confidential, anonymous questionnaire. We ask that no names, including those of bullies, your child, or staff members are used.

Please have your child complete this survey with you. (You may wish to have younger children dictate their responses.) Please respect your child's answers and refrain from editing or directing their replies to these questions.

**FOR STUDENTS**

• Are there places you feel safe at our school? ❏ Yes ❏ No   Where are they?

• Are there places you feel unsafe at our school? ❏ Yes ❏ No   Where are they?

• What is a bully?

• What things might help you if you were being bullied?

• What consequences do you think there should be for bullies?

**FOR PARENTS**

• Do you see bullying as a major problem at our school? Why or why not?

• If your family had experiences with bullying previously at our school, how was it dealt with?

• What areas do you think a school-wide bully-proofing focus should include?

• What consequences do you feel would be appropriate for children who bully?

*We thank you for your input, and look forward to sharing our plans with you in upcoming weeks.*

---

framework makes it easier for parents to understand the program's purpose and parameters—and they may be more willing to improve the existing structure than suggest a new approach.

Be very clear about how parent's opinions, concerns, and expectations will be addressed; as with staff, parents must realize that the final policy will be developed by the administrative team and will strive to be respectful and fair to all. If there are no clear parameters in place, some parents may expect that their strong opinions and expectations will be clearly evident in the final result. Care must be taken to implement policies that will work for *all* students and staff.

Parents will be pleased that the school is addressing the issue of bullying in an organized way. The purpose of this data-gathering is two-fold; by gathering important information, you understand whether parents think the school is currently addressing the issues of bullying adequately and in what direction school policies need to go. It also gives you an opportunity to understand the perceptions of your school both from staff and the community at large. This is a chance for the administration and staff to create excitement and a commitment to this new policy.

## 4 Developing a School-Wide Plan

Now that there is a clear picture about your school's policy and you have considered the response from parents and students, your school's staff must assess how these policies need to be adjusted. Staff may meet in teams and have a representative report back to the administrative team or the entire staff may gather to answer the guiding questions listed at right. Following the meeting, a smaller team of teachers and administrators can use these ideas to draft a policy.

It's important for *all* staff to be involved in setting and following the guidelines. Support-staff members are often overlooked when policies about bullying are made, yet they are usually the people most closely involved with bullying incidents. Since bullying tends to take place in unstructured situations such as the lunchroom, playground, or school bus, their input is invaluable. Support staff may also be more willing to support and follow a clear policy they've helped develop.

Staff training in handling bullying situations is also essential; every person has a different understanding of the problem, and may approach

> **GUIDING QUESTIONS:**
> - What are the areas that have been targeted for improvement?
> - What kind of school atmosphere should be created and how can this be achieved?
> - What will be the "nuts-and-bolts" of the school's bully-proofing policy?
> - How will the school support bullied children? What are the parameters for working with bullies?
> - How will the administrative team make sure that all staff members understand and follow the guidelines?

**CHAPTER 8**

bullying incidents with different skill-levels. Some helpful staff development sessions you might recommend include guest speakers who can provide information about bullying, teachers from other schools with effective programs, films or videos on the subject, or using the activities and discussion questions in this book. Attending these together will help your staff gain a common understanding of the issue.

A bully-proofing plan will not be successful unless every staff member supports and follows it.

As your school-wide plan begins to take shape, each staff member needs a clear understanding of his or her role and the expectations for that role within the school's bully-free framework. What will he or she do first? What kinds of consequences can he or she try? What is the next step? The plan logistics must be clearly thought-out and discussed in advance, which is why it's helpful for each staff and support staff member in the school to have developed a personal action plan. (See Chapter 2 for a sample plan for teachers.) Administrators also need to take the time to devise their own plans so that they have a predictable series of actions to follow when a staff member refers a student who has repeatedly bullied other students. The more specific the plan the more effectively the situation can be handled. When each staff member implements a bully-proofing plan in his or her area, he or she supports the school-wide effort and is on the same page as the rest of the school community.

Another major component of the school-wide program should be conflict resolution, and appropriate training must be in place so that all staff members can use it consistently in their own classrooms, and during other supervisory activities. Introduce these in much the same way as you would to students (see Chapter 7 for details). You may find it effective and useful to have students familiar with conflict resolution role-play scenarios for staff.

**A SAMPLE SCHOOL-WIDE PLAN**

The Bullying Incident Report form can be saved on a computer that is easily accessible to all staff members or photocopied forms can be placed in a binder with sheets of carbon paper to make quick copies. A professional print shop can also create carbon-embedded booklets of forms for use. A sample reproducible report form appears on page 106.

Once each staff member has a personal plan for how he or she can respond to bullying, it is appropriate to draft a school plan. A typical school plan is outlined on page 105. Note that the first part of this plan focuses attention on the bully and the second part addresses the needs of bullied children. These children, particularly if they are targeted repeatedly, require just as much attention as the bully.

This plan includes an important record-keeping tool, the Bullying Incident Report, which helps staff members record critical information about every bullying incident in a consistent manner. Completed forms can be kept in a binder in the office. A reproducible form is included on page 106.

## Bully-Free School Plan

**PART A    RESPONDING TO BULLIES**

### 1. Bullying Incident:

a. Nearest staff member deals immediately with incident, following personal action plan.

b. Staff member uses conflict resolution framework and applies an appropriate consequence.

c. Staff member documents the incident, using the Bullying Incident Report form located in office; one copy stays in office binder, one copy in teacher's mailbox.

d. Principal or administrative team member checks binder forms regularly and monitors bullying incidents, providing support to staff when necessary.

### 2. Repeated Bullying:

Follow steps 1–3 above. When a student has three forms, the principal becomes involved and homeroom teacher is notified.

**The principal:**

a. immediately discusses the incident with the student, follows personal plan and applies appropriate consequence.

b. calls parents or guardian of bullying student.

c. keeps official documentation; copies of all behavior forms included along with detailed plan of action in a student file.

d. uses one or more of the following strategies if problem continues: meets with parents and student, refers to School Resource Team, enters student into mentoring program, meets with teacher to set up detailed plan of action.

**PART B    RESPONDING TO BULLIED CHILDREN**

### 1. Bullying Incident:

Nearest staff member follows step 1, a–c in Part A. (Staff member should clearly indicate on the Bullying Incident Report form what role each child played.)

### 2. Repeated Bullying:

As soon as a child has been bullied twice, principal becomes involved and homeroom teacher is notified.

**The principal:**

a. meets immediately with child to discuss the incident.

b. calls parents or guardian of bullied student.

c. meets with teacher and parents to draw up action plan.

d. coaches child on additional bully-proofing strategies.

e. in concert with teacher, monitors progress weekly.

**The teacher:**

a. follows his or her personal bully-proofing plan to support the bullied child. (Personal coaching; review bully-proofing strategies.)

# BULLYING INCIDENT REPORT

Date: _____

Staff member involved: _____

Students involved: _____

* Homeroom teacher(s): _____

Place incident occurred: ❐ playground  ❐ lunchroom  ❐ bus  ❐ classroom  ❐ other (specify)

_____

Brief description of incident: _____

_____

_____

_____

_____

Conflict resolution framework used:  ❐ Yes   ❐ No

Consequence agreed upon: _____

_____

_____

_____

_____

Follow–up needed: _____

Comments: _____

_____

_____

_____

_____

*Copies to be placed in the mailbox of each homeroom teacher named above.

A key part of the plan is for the principal and administrative team to be very involved in dealing with the problem. When a bully realizes that his or her behavior is being monitored by a team including teachers, the principal, and his or her parents, bullying behaviors tend to decrease significantly. As well, the child learns that the school takes the negative behavior seriously and consequences will be applied every time there is a problem. "Consequences are consistent, clear, and unavoidable" is an apt slogan for any school team with a good plan in place.

Developing appropriate consequences deserves time and attention. As discussed in Chapter 3, consequences are an essential ingredient in any classroom and school. Sometimes, the differences between punishment and consequences can be confusing, especially to those unused to the idea of logical consequences. Make sure your staff discusses the definition of each and develops a list of appropriate consequences that mesh with your school's standards of behavior. The list of consequences becomes a meaningful, useful tool for all staff, and ensures consistency. Use the list on page 39 to get started. Remember, don't do something because it's the way it's always been done; try new approaches to solving the problem.

## 5 Inviting Student Input Into School-Wide Rules

Once students become aware of the school-wide standards of behavior, have them participate in developing school rules and behavior expectations. Children who are asked to help create appropriate rules for the school are more likely to take ownership of them—and follow them. This, in turn, supports your bully-free program. Some ideas for eliciting student input follow.

Each class might be asked to submit one simple rule. Each should clearly relate to the school's standards, such as Respect: "Speak to other people politely; never yell." When you develop the final list, be sure to limit the number and complexity of the rules or they may become so unmanageable that no one will pay any attention. Students may vote on five or ten top rules to finalize the list.

These rules should then be clearly displayed throughout the school and in each classroom. Each class might create the display for a rule—the more eye-catching the better! Ideas for the display include:

- a wall mural demonstrating each rule.

- hand-painted cloth banners running across a hallway with one rule on each.

- in the main hallway, a line of oversized paper T-shirts hung on a clothesline (use clothespins) under the banner "Rules That Make It Great to Hang Around Our School." Each T-shirt might have a rule printed on it.

Displays like these encourage children to study the rules. In addition, they provide a colorful atmosphere, create a welcoming feel, and most important, ensure that every child and adult in the school knows the rules; it's hard to plead ignorance when you are standing under a huge banner with the rules written on it!

## 6 The Importance of a Positive School Atmosphere

When a school is an exciting, positive place to be, students tend to respect the rules and actively engage in productive activities. The best way to help bullies and bullied children feel that they are a valuable part of the school community is to create opportunities for them, and all children, to participate in events that are enjoyable for everyone. Special events bring people together. I have included the ones that I have found most successful.

During these activities, the school's standards of behavior, along with any expectations for behaviors specific to the activity, should always be clearly defined and maintained. Some activities can lead to chaos if there are no parameters in place; make following the rules an essential ingredient in taking part in the fun.

Consider these ways to create a positive school atmosphere and an awareness of the behavior standards you expect. Some ideas include:

- fifth- and sixth-grade leadership groups.

- buddy programs (primary and upper grades pair up and take part in activities together throughout the year).

- spirit days (for example, in a Backward Day, everyone goes through the day's schedule backward. People may wear clothing backward and eat dessert first at lunch—students love activities like this. These special days are often a great way for all students to feel involved, have fun, and share a positive experience.).

- guest speaker assemblies (local authors, bullying specialists).

- rotating activities led by students and teachers from each grade level who form a "house" within the school community (for example, the third grade "house" conducts races at recess).

- community projects (your school plants and maintains a garden on your school grounds, or older students write a community history by interviewing senior citizens).

- a peer mediators program for the playground.

- assemblies that support the themes of Respect, Tolerance, and Empathy.

Creating a Bully-Free Classroom • Scholastic Teaching Resources

# 7 Communicating School Policies Effectively

Once your school staff has set up a school-wide plan to deal with repeated bullying incidents, you'll want to share the plan with students and parents.

Of course, communicating these policies and rules to students and parents clearly, concisely, and consistently is essential. Class meetings led by teachers are a helpful way to introduce rules and activities to children. Daily announcements reminding students of the standards or noting positive behaviors that administrators have witnessed in hallways and classrooms (anonymous of course) are helpful, but you must make sure these announcements are interesting to listen to. "Riddle of the Day" or simple contests ("The first five people who can find the new display in the main hallway *and* tell me the slogan will win a comic book") really help motivate students to pay attention.

Special newsletters or a regular column in your school's monthly newsletter are great ways of involving and informing parents; if you can include a contest or interactive activity for parents and children to respond to, so much the better. Finding creative ways of presenting the information will catch parents' attention and ensure they read what you send home.

# 8 Taking a Proactive Approach to Bullying

Once you have a policy clearly spelled out, and staff fully participating, don't sit back and wait for a problem; take a proactive stance to minimize bullying in your school. This might include having teachers (and administrators) present in the hallway as children enter or leave classrooms—not necessarily to police children but to greet them or wave them off at the end of the day. For administrators, it pays dividends to learn every child's name. It's a big deal for a child to be greeted personally by the principal in a pleasant, "I've-noticed-you-and-I'm-glad-you're-here-today" kind of way. The positive tone resonates through the school.

Having caring adults interact with individual students is part of another proactive strategy— targeting children who are bullies on a school-wide basis. Administrators can bring all staff on

---

**FOSTERING POSITIVE RELATIONSHIPS BETWEEN ADMINISTRATORS AND STUDENTS**

Some ideas to help foster a positive relationship:

- Have lunch with the child outside and do some bird-watching.

- Teach the child a new hobby such as building a model or painting-by-numbers.

- Solve a jigsaw puzzle by working together.

- Do a science experiment that interests the child.

- Teach an older child how to work the AV equipment or microphone; have the student assist you in setting up for an assembly.

- Read a favorite book together (you may find some appropriate choices on pages 111–112).

**CHAPTER 8**

board to closely monitor and support the growth of a repeat offender. Too often, children who bully and those with other behavior problems expect only negative responses from adults. By noticing and supporting these children regularly, consistently, and kindly, we may help bullies begin to feel that they are worthwhile, likeable people. Such modeling can help reshape their behavior.

While teachers need to be involved in this process, it is the administration that must take a lead role in this area. Most often, bullies only deal with the principal when they are in trouble. However, ongoing, consistent and positive attention from the principal can have a huge impact on a student's behavior and connection to the school.

Whatever you do, it must be enjoyable for both of you. Make sure that each activity is interactive; watching a video together means you both lose the opportunity to learn about each other. Tutoring a child in a subject area should be kept for another time, unless it is something the student genuinely wants to do. Set your intention on helping the child feel that he or she is important to you, and is capable and valued. Talk, laugh, tell jokes—give him or her the opportunity to be involved in a positive way at school.

> It's important for bullies to realize that they will still be held accountable for their behavior and face consequences each time they are involved in bullying, even if the principal is their mentor. Of course, dealing with the consequences of their behavior with someone whom they like, and who likes them, may have a deep impact on children. Knowing that they've let someone down who believes in them can be a humbling experience.

Of course, the mentoring process works equally well for bullied children. They, too, deserve the opportunity to be supported and feel that an adult in the school other than their teacher really knows and cares about them.

All students need to feel that they are valued and appreciated. They have a right to feel safe and know that all staff members will support them if they are bullied. A comprehensive bully-free policy, carefully thought through, implemented consistently, and clearly communicated to students and parents goes a long way toward making school a safe and welcoming learning community for children.

# Recommended Children's Literature to Support the "Big Four"

*These resources support the concepts taught in each unit of your bully-free plan (Chapters 3–7).*

## NO MORE BULLIES! (BULLY PROOFING)

Agassi, M. (2000). *Hands Are Not for Hitting.* Minneapolis, MN: Free Spirit Press. (Grades 1–2).

Amos, J. (1994). *It's Your Choice: Bully.* New York: Benchmark Books. (Grades 1–3).

Berenstain, S. (2001). *Berenstain Bears: The Wrong Crowd.* New York: Random House. (Grades 1–3).

Best, C. (2001). *Shrinking Violet.* New York: Farrar, Straus and Giroux. (Grades 1–3).

Boyd, L. (1989). *Bailey the Big Bully.* New York: Viking Kestrel. (Grades 1–3).

Brimner, L. D. (1990). *Cory Coleman, Grade Two.* New York: Holt. (Grades 1–3).

Brown, M. (1983). *Arthur's April Fool.* New York: Little, Brown. (Grades 1–3).

Byars, B. (1973). *The 18ᵗʰ Emergency.* New York: Viking Kestrel. (Grade 3).

Carrick, C. (1983). *What a Wimp.* New York: Clarion. (Grades 2–3).

Caseley, J. (2001). *Bully.* New York: Greenwillow. (Grades 1–3).

Clements, A. (2001). *Jake Drake, Bully Buster.* New York: Simon & Schuster. (Grades 2–3).

Cosby, B. (1997). *The Meanest Thing to Say.* New York: Scholastic. (Grades 1–2).

Couric, K. (2000). *The Brand-New Kid.* New York: Doubleday. (Grades 1–3).

Cox, J. (1999). *Mean, Mean Maureen Green.* New York: Holiday House. (Grades 1–3).

dePaola, T. (1979). *Oliver Button Is a Sissy.* Orlando, FL: Harcourt Brace Jovanovich. (Grades 1–3).

Estes, E. (1972). *The Hundred Dresses.* Orlando, FL: Harcourt, Brace. (Grades 2–3).

Howe, J. (1996). *Pinky and Rex and the Bully.* New York: Atheneum. (Grades 1–3).

Johnston, M. (1996). *Dealing With Insults.* New York: Power Kids Press. (Grades 1–2).

Jonell, L. (2002). *Bravemole.* New York: GP Putnam and Sons. (Grades 1–3).

Levy, E. (1998). *Third Grade Bullies.* New York: Hyperion. (Grade 3).

Little, J. (1991). *Jess Was the Brave One.* New York: Viking. (Grades 1–3).

McCain, B. (2001). *Nobody Knew What to Do.* Morton Grove, IL: Albert Whitman & Co. (Grades 1–3).

Naylor, P. (1991). *King of the Playground.* New York: Atheneum. (Grades 1–3).

O'Neill, A. (2002). *Mean Jean, the Recess Queen.* New York: Scholastic. (Grades 1–3).

Sanders, P. (1996). *What Do You Know About Bullying?* Brookfield, CT: Copper Beech Books. (Grades 2–3).

Smallcomb, P. (2002). *Camp Buccaneer.* New York: Simon & Schuster. (Grades 1–3).

Stolz, M. (1963). *The Bully of Barkham Street.* New York: HarperCollins. (Grades 2–3).

Wells, R. (1973). *Benjamin and Tulip.* New York: Dial. (Grades 1–3).

Williams, K. L. (1992). *First Grade King.* New York: Clarion. (Grades 1–2).

Winthrop, E. (1990). *Luke's Bully.* New York: Viking. (Grade 3).

Zolotow, C. (1969). *The Hating Book.* New York: Harper and Row. (Grades 1–3).

## MARVELOUS ME! (BUILDING SELF-ESTEEM AND CONFIDENCE)

Anholt, C. & L. (1995). *What Makes Me Happy?* Cambridge, MA: Candlewick Press. (Grades 1–3).

Appelt, K. (2003). *Incredible Me!* New York: HarperCollins. (Grades 1–3).

Harper, C. M. (2001). *When I Grow Up.* San Francisco: Chronicle Books. (Grades 1–3).

Kaufman, G., R., & L. & Espeland, P. (1999). *Stick Up for Yourself: Every Kid's Guide to Personal Power and Positive Self-Esteem.* Minneapolis, MN: Free Spirit. (Grade 3).

Zolotow, C. (1963). *The Quarrelling Book.* New York: HarperCollins. (Grades 1–3).

## FABULOUS FRIENDS

Albregts, L. & Cape, E. (1998). *Best Friends: Tons of Crazy, Cool Things to Do With Your Girlfriends.* Chicago: Review Press. (Grades 1–3).

Bloom, P. (1999). *Best Friends, A Special True Book about Friendship.* Boston: Element Books. (Grade 3).

Bourgeois, P. (1998). *Franklin's Secret Club.* Toronto: Kids Can Press. (Grades 1–3).

Brenner, B. (1992). *Group Soup.* New York: Viking. (Grade 1).

Brown, L. K. & M. C. (1998). *How to Be a Friend.* New York: Little, Brown. (Grades 1–2).

Cohen, M. (1971). *Best Friends.* New York: MacMillan. (Grade 1)

Cowan-Fletcher, J. (1994). *It Takes a Village.* New York: Scholastic. (Grades 1–3).

Griff, P. R. (1988). *B-E-S-T Friends.* New York: Bantam Doubleday. (Grades 1–3).

Hoff, S. (1985). *Who Will Be My Friends?* New York: HarperCollins. (Grades 1–2).

Kellogg, S. (1986). *Best Friends.* New York: Dial. (Grades 1–3).

Leedy, L. (1996). *How Humans Make Friends.* New York: Holiday House. (Grades 1–3).

Levete, S. (1998). *How Do I Feel About. . . Making Friends.* Brookfield, CT: Copper Beech Books. (Grades 1–3).

Pilkey, Dav. (1991). *A Friend for Dragon.* New York: Orchard Books. (Grades 1–3).

Rogers, F. (1987). *Making Friends.* New York: Putnam and Sons. (Grades 1–2).

Ross, D. (1999). *A Book of Friends.* New York: HarperCollins. (Grades 1–3).

Scott, E. (2000). *Friends.* New York: Atheneum. (Grades 1–3).

Wells, R. (2003). *Make New Friends.* New York: Hyperion (Grades 1-3).

Weninger, B. (1999). *Why Are You Fighting, Davy?* New York: North-South Books. (Grades 1–3).

## CONFLICT RESOLUTION

Crary, E. (2001). *Amy's Disappearing Pickle.* Seattle: Parenting Press. (Grades 1–3).

Crary, E. (2001). *I Want It.* Seattle: Parenting Press. (Grades 1–3).

Simmons, J. (2003). *Seeing Red: An Anger Management and Peacemaking Curriculum for Kids.* British Columbia, Canada: New Society Publishers. (Grades 1–3).

Whitehouse, E. & Warwick P. (1996). *A Volcano in My Tummy.* British Columbia, Canada: New Society Publishers. (Grades 1–3).

Zehler, A. (2001). *Two Fine Ladies Have a Tiff.* New York: Random House. (Grade 1).

# Professional Sources Cited

Adams, H. (1994). *Peace in the Classroom.* Winnipeg, Canada: Peguis Publishers.

Banks, R. (March 1997). Bullying in Schools. Power of One Foundation. Available: http://www.powerof onefoundation.org/Bullying%20in%20Schools-Ron%20Banks.htm

Beran, T. & Tutty, L. M. (2001, April). Elementary Students' Reports of Bullying and Safety at School. *Canadian Journal of School Psychology.*

Bullying (2001, March). *American Academy of Child and Adolescent Psychiatry* (no. 8). Available: http://www.aacap.org/publications/factsfam/80.htm

Caldwell, A. (2004, April 20). Columbine: A recurring nightmare. *The Denver Post.*

Coloroso, B. (2003). *The Bully, the Bullied, and the Bystander.* New York: HarperResource.

Dedman, B. (2000, October 15). Deadly lessons: School shooters: Secret Service findings. *Chicago Sun-Times.*

Garrity, C. (1998). *Bully-Proofing Your School.* Longmont, CO: Sopris West.

Preventing School Shootings: A Summary of a U.S. Secret Service Safe School Initiative Report, 2000. (2002). *National Institute of Justice Journal* (no.248). Available: http://www.ncjrs.org/pdffiles1 /jr000248c.pdf

Romain, Trevor. (1997). *Bullies Are a Pain in the Brain.* Minneapolis, MN: Free Spirit Publishing.

Teolis, B. (1998). *Ready-to-Use Conflict Resolution Activities.* West Nyack, NY: Center for Applied Research in Education.

Creating a Bully-Free Classroom • Scholastic Teaching Resources